FRIDTJOF NANSEN AND THE GREEK REFUGEE CRISIS
1922–1924

*A Study on the Politics of International Humanitarian Intervention
and the Greek-Turkish Obligatory Population Exchange Agreement*

# Fridtjof Nansen and the Greek Refugee Crisis 1922–1924

A STUDY ON THE POLITICS OF
INTERNATIONAL HUMANITARIAN INTERVENTION
AND THE GREEK-TURKISH OBLIGATORY
POPULATION EXCHANGE AGREEMENT

## Harry J. Psomiades

*Professor Emeritus of Political Science*
*The City University of New York*

THE ASIA MINOR AND PONTOS HELLENIC RESEARCH CENTER
Bloomingdale, Illinois

FRIDTJOF NANSEN AND THE GREEK REFUGEE CRISIS
1922–1924

A Study on the Politics of International Humanitarian Intervention
and the Greek-Turkish Obligatory Population Exchange Agreement

Library of Congress Control Number 2011916197

ISBN 978-1-4507-9241-7

THE ASIA MINOR AND PONTOS
HELLENIC RESEARCH CENTER
P.O. BOX 6127
Bloomingdale, IL 60108-6127

PRINTED IN THE UNITED STATES OF AMERICA
BY
ATHENS PRINTING COMPANY
337 West 36th Street
New York, NY 10018-6401

To my wife Maria Vassiliou
Founder and President
of the Human Rights Defence Centre (Athens)

# Abbreviations

AMAE    France, *Archives du Ministère des Affaires Étrangères*, Series "E", 1919–1929 (Paris)

BFSP    Great Britain, Foreign Office, *British and Foreign State Papers* (London)

DBFP    Great Britain, Foreign Office. *Documents on British Foreign Policy,1919–1939* (London)

DDI     Italy, Ministero degli Affari Esteri. *I Documenti Diplomatici Italiani* (Rome)

FRUS    The United States, *Papers Relating to the Foreign Relations of the United States* (Washington, D.C.)

AYE     Greece. *The Diplomatic and Historical Archives of the Hellenic Ministry of Foreign Affairs* (Athens)

LCNEA   Great Britain, *Parliamentary Papers.1923, Turkey.* No.1, Cmd. 1814. "*Lausanne Conference on Near Eastern Affairs, 1922–1923*" (Proceedings), 1923, London

LNOJ    League of Nations, *Official Journal* (Geneva).

RICR    The International Red Cross, *Revue International la Croix-Rouge* (Geneva)

# Contents

# Preface

This study has its roots in previous publications of the author on Greek-Turkish relations, which are listed in the bibliography. Over the years, I have used with much profit the appropriate foreign policy archives in London, Paris, Rome, and Washington D.C. for my studies on Greek-Turkish relations. Regrettably, the Ottoman and Turkish Nationalist archives for the period of this study still remain closed to the public. All dates are given in accordance with the Gregorian or "Western" calendar, which is 13 days ahead of the Julian or "old" calendar. Greece officially adopted the new style Gregorian calendar on March 1, 1923.

I would like to acknowledge that this work was also made possible, in part, by a grant from the Alexander S. Onassis Public Benefit Foundation; by the support of the director, Dr. Ursula-Maria Ruser, and staff of the League of Nations Archives, the Library and Office of the United Nations (Geneva); by the director, Dr. Valentini Tselika, and staff of the Benaki Museum Historical Archives, Penelope Delta House (Kifisia); by the director, Dr. Photini Thomai Constatopoulou, and staff, especially Michael Mantios, of the Diplomatic and Historical Archives, Hellenic Ministry of Foreign Affairs (Athens); by the director, I.K. Mazarakis-Ainian, and staff of the National Historical Museum (Athens); and to Dr. Stavros Anestides for his help and hospitality at the Centre of Asia Minor Studies (Athens).

The author and publisher are grateful for the permission of the United Nations Library, Picture Collection (Geneva) to reproduce the cover photograph of a portrait of Dr. Fridtjof Nansen made by the Norwegian artist, Axel Revold (1946), which is mounted in Geneva's Palais des Nations. It is a reminder to those who visit there, of Nansen's extraordinary achievements in the service of the League of Nations and humanity amid the rubble and tragedy of the crushed hopes and dreams of millions of souls after a decade of global war and revolution.

I owe a special debt to Professor Theodore A. Couloumbis for his detailed and insightful critique of my work; to Professor George Giannakopoulos for his intimate knowledge of the Greek refugee crisis and for his support in the preparation of my manuscript for publication; to Christine Psomiades Eames for her editorial support; and to George Shirinian for his acute attention to detail as editor-in-chief in the final preparation of the text. I also owe special thanks to the members of the Asia Minor and Pontos Hellenic Research Center in Bloomingdale, Illinois, and to its extraordinary President, George Mavropoulos, for their valuable support and sponsorship of the publication of this volume.

My immediate obligations are to my wife, Maria Vassiliou, for her invaluable critical review of my manuscript. Her unwavering support and advice have been a constant source of encouragement for the completion of this project. Needless to say, I assume sole responsibility for the views and opinions expressed herein.

H.J.P.

# Prologue

Why did all of the participants at the Lausanne conference for a Near East peace, 1922–1923, find it necessary to accept the principle of a compulsory rather than a voluntary exchange of populations between Greece and Turkey as a solution to the Greek refugee crisis? Why had all the delegates at Lausanne expressed their deep misgiving and concern over the legitimacy and morality of a forced population exchange but at the same time agreed to its passage? Indeed, their open and unanimous condemnation of the principle of coercion as being unjust and bereft of human dignity must largely explain their denial of any responsibility for its paternity. Yet, at the same time, they all backed the agreement, although none wished to sponsor it openly. Was it yet another case of a constant condition in politics involving the clash between pragmatism and principles, between perceived national interests and the emerging international obligation of humanitarian intervention?

For the first time in human history, the participants at Lausanne were establishing the principle of the involuntary displacement of populations as an international norm. The violation of the basic human right of choice, the uprooting of people from their ancestral homes, with no say in the matter, had to be viewed as a regressive step in relations between nations. The Greek-Turkish compulsory population exchange agreement could not be justified on legal or moral grounds.

Why, therefore, had the responsible governments at Lausanne consented to the principle of an obligatory exchange of populations, even before the opening of the peace conference on November 21, 1922? Was there an alternative? Why did they depart from the precedent of a voluntary exchange? Why did they go along with the notion that the only way to deal with areas of mixed populations was to "unmix" them? What motivated the interested parties to reach this conclusion? Should we infer their motives for supporting the popu-

1

lation exchange from the ultimate benefits it produced for peace and stability in the region? The answers to these and other related questions are a major focus of this study, keeping in mind that in diplomacy, the players have the capacity of holding contradictory opinions and that there is often disharmony between their official pronouncements and actual policies. The researcher must then ask whether or not it is a case of the players obfuscating their real intentions or reconsidering their assumptions and positions due to a swiftly shifting political reality.

Paradoxically, two men in this Greek tragedy, who were least able to alter the course of events, were the ones to receive the most criticism for supporting the obligatory exchange of populations. More fingers were pointed at them than at any one else for suggesting that the exchange be compulsory. They were the famous Norwegian arctic explorer and scholar, Dr. Fridtjof Nansen, special envoy of the League of Nations and its first High Commissioner for Refugees; and the veteran Greek statesman and former prime minister of Greece, Eleftherios Venizelos, newly appointed by the Greek Revolutionary Government to represent Greek interests abroad and to act as chief of the Greek delegation at Lausanne. There is near unanimous agreement that the influence of Nansen on the negotiations and terms of reference, which led to a final settlement to the Greek refugee crisis, was decisive, despite the fact that he represented an embryonic League of Nations whose field of action was largely limited by the Great Powers. The imprint of Venizelos in these proceedings was also deemed pivotal despite the fact that he represented a defeated and impoverished Greece that had to bear the primary burden of the compulsory exchange. Their success can best be explained by their remarkable leadership qualities, by their celebrity status and reputation, and by their skill and considerable experience as negotiators.

This study will also give special attention to the interactions between these two men and their role as central actors in a refugee crisis of massive proportions. It will attempt, in part, to respond to the criticism that Nansen had allowed the Powers to exploit his role as an international civil servant in order to legitimize their solution to the

Greek refugee problem.[1] And that Venizelos had a preconceived plan to take advantage of the refugee situation, using the refugees as a pawn to secure financial aid for the economic reconstruction of his country and/or that he championed a compulsory exchange, primarily to secure Greece's northern provinces—as an innovation for peace.[2]

*Shifting Frontiers and Population Exchanges in the Balkans and Anatolia, 1912–1922*

Prior to the 20th century, the phrase "population exchange" did not exist in the language of European diplomacy. Goods and prisoners were exchanged but not innocent civilians. Of course, there have always been movements of populations within and beyond a state's borders, voluntary and involuntary, throughout recorded history. Territorial shifts were often accompanied by population shifts. But it was not until after the Thirty Years War in the seventeenth century that attempts were made to provide some rules in European public law for the rights of populations living in ceded territories following major wars. Initially, the practice was to impose the nationality of the victor on the inhabitants of the conquered territories. Later, however, at least since the Treaty of Utrecht of 1713, it became accepted practice to afford the populations of these territories the choice (the optional clause) of either continuing to live in them, but vacating their former nationality; or quitting the territories and keeping their former nationality. But they were also afforded the right, in theory at least, to freely dispose of their property. This right was to be seen by many as an encouragement to hasten the departure of an unwanted population. But it also recognized in modern parlance that the right to property was a human right. However, those living in multiethnic states, where sovereignty remained unaltered, did not have this right.[3] This was soon to change.

---

[1] Roland Huntford, *Nansen: The Explorer as Hero* (London: Abacus, 1997), p. 530.

[2] John A. Petropulos, "The Compulsory Exchange of Populations: Greek-Turkish Peacemaking, 1922–1930," *Byzantine and Modern Greek Studies* 2 (1976): 137.

[3] For a detailed discussion on the origins of international accords relating to the exchange of populations see Stelios Seferiades, *L'échange des populations* (Paris: Hachette, 1929), pp. 44–64.

The notion of an officially sanctioned exchange of populations as a solution to political tensions had its origins in the Balkans. As a result of the Balkan Wars of 1912–1913 and their aftermath, the first wave of needy Christian and Muslim refugees cascaded across the newly delineated frontiers to seek refuge in their respective "motherland." From the times of the Balkan Wars, the vast majority of the refugees were not surprisingly Muslims, some 300,000. They were driven out of Macedonia and Thrace primarily by Serbian or Bulgarian forces. Some 60,000 were pushed out of or left voluntarily Greek Macedonia. In 1914–1915, the vast majority of the refugees, some 200,000 were primarily Ottoman Greeks pushed out of the Ottoman territories of Eastern Thrace and western Anatolia.[4] These movements further exacerbated nationalist feelings and set in motion population exchange agreements between Bulgaria and Turkey, Greece and Turkey, and following Bulgaria's defeat in World War I, between Greece and Bulgaria.[5] These agreements understandably influenced the decision makers at Lausanne.

A protocol between Bulgaria and Turkey following the Treaty of Bucharest (August 10, 1913), which brought to an end the Second Balkan War, was annexed to the Treaty of Constantinople (September 29, 1913) between the Ottoman Empire and Bulgaria.[6] It not only included the optional clause but was the first interstate treaty in history providing for and using the expression "an exchange of populations." The optional clause was also inserted in the Treaty of Athens (November 14, 1913) between Greece and the Ottoman Empire. The

[4]A.J. Toynbee, *The Western Question in Greece and Turkey* (London: Constable and Co., 1922), p. 138; A.A.Pallis, "Racial Migrations in the Balkans during the Years 1912–1924," *Geographical Journal* 66 no. 4 (October 1925), and his "The Exchange of Populations in the Balkans," *The Nineteenth Century and After* 47 (March 1925): 1–8; and *The Historical Archives of the Greek Ministry of Foreign Affairs* (hereafter cited as *AYE*), 1914: A.A.K. 17 & 26. In 1912 there were approximately 2 million Ottoman Greeks in Eastern Thrace, Constantinople, the Pontos, and Asia Minor, some 8–9 million Ottoman Muslims/Turks and at least 1.7 million Ottoman Armenians.

[5]C 186 (1922), League of Nations Archives, Nansen Papers, Vol. IV. Commission Mixte d'Emigration Greco-Bulgare. Procès-Verbaux de la Commission 1921–1922. Annex, 61st Session, 21 Septembre 1921. Première Partie. *Historique sommaire des déplacements successifs de frontières et des migration de populations entre l'Empire Ottoman, la Grèce et la Bulgarie depuis 1900.*

[6]Great Britain, Foreign Office, *British and Foreign State Papers,* 107, pp. 713–714.

Ottoman treaty with Bulgaria was implemented by an accord on November 15, 1913, providing for a limited voluntary exchange of Bulgarians and Muslims living in a 15 kilometer zone on each side of their common border in Thrace. But it was basically a recognition of an accomplished fact, since most of the people involved had already fled from these zones during the upheavals of the Balkan Wars. The Ottoman-Bulgarian treaty, however, did allow an effective means of forcing the transfer of the few remaining groups left on the defeated side of the border. The Turkish government was particularly set on expelling its Bulgarian minority whose property was being sequestered by Muslim refugees from Western Thrace. In all, approximately 48,500 Muslims moved from Bulgarian territory to Turkey compared to 46,700 Bulgarians who left, for the most part unwillingly, for Bulgaria from Turkish Thrace.[7] Thus, the Bulgarian chamber refused to ratify the accord. Although the principle of the optional clause was reaffirmed, it was not a voluntary exchange of population.[8] The more germane accord, also initiated by Turkey, was that between Greece and Turkey eight months later, although it was never ratified because of Turkey's entry in World War I on November 1, 1914. Briefly, it was sparked by the systematic persecution, harassment, and forced exodus of the Ottoman Greeks from Eastern Thrace and from the Aegean coast of Asia Minor. The reasons for the expulsions were three-fold: (1) The influx of the Balkan Muslim refugees naturally led to reprisals against the numerous Ottoman Greek communities in Eastern Thrace and western Anatolia. They were being evicted from their homes by the Muslim refugees with the acquiescence and active support of the state; (2) The further implementation of the policy of Turkification by the Young Turks, particularly by the ruling Committee of Union and Progress (CUP), which directed an organized system of harassment and intimidation to eliminate or clear out the Christian population of all of Thrace and the Turkish Aegean coast and replace them with Muslim immigrants

[7]Harry J. Psomiades, *The Eastern Question: The Last Phase. A Study in Greek-Turkish Diplomacy* (Thessaloniki: Institute for Balkan Studies, 1968), p. 55.
[8]Seferiades, *L'échange des populations*, p. 48.

from the Balkans and the Russian Empire; (3) The decision on February 16, 1914, by the six Powers—Germany, Austria-Hungary, France, Britain, Russia, and Italy—to assign to Greece the eastern Aegean islands. These islands had been occupied by Greece during the Balkan Wars. Needless to say, the decision was unacceptable to Turkey for reasons of security.[9] It refused to recognize Greek sovereignty over the Greek populated islands, particularly Mitylene, Chios, and Samos, because of their strategic location just of the Anatolian coast, with its large Ottoman Greek population centers.[10] The Ottoman policy of persecution and eviction was designed in part to put pressure on Athens to reach an agreement with the Sultan's Government or the Sublime Porte on the disposition of the islands.

In response to the protests of the Greek government and its demands for the cessation of hostilities toward the Ottoman Greek population, the Sublime Porte recommended a population exchange of the Greek rural population of Eastern Thrace and the Aydin province or *vilayet*, including the Smyrna district, for the Muslim rural population of Greek Macedonia and Epiros. On May 18, 1914, the Turkish minister in Athens, Ghalib Kemaly [Söylemezoğlu], wrote to the Greek premier, Eleftherious Venizelos: "During our last conversation I brought forward to you as a personal opinion the idea of making an exchange of the Greek rural population of the vilayet of Smyrna with the Muslims of Macedonia. Having submitted this idea for the approval of the Sublime Porte, I have the pleasure of making known to you that it agrees with the idea. I now make the proposal officially in the name of my Government."[11] He warned Venizelos on several occasions that only by accepting the population exchange would there be peace in the Orient.[12]

---

[9]These Greek populated islands were occupied by Greece during the first Balkan War, which was terminated by the Treaty of London, May 30, 1913.

[10]Djemal Pasha, *Memories of a Turkish Statesman, 1913–1919* (London: Hutchinson, 1924), p. 55.

[11]*AYE*, 1914: A.A.K. 28

[12]As told in a brochure by Ghalib Kemaly published in Rome in 1919 and found in *Venizelos Papers*, 24. Coromilas (Rome) to Venizelos (Paris), November 23, 1919; Three years later in an interview with a Turkish journalist, Ghalib Kemaly insisted that it was Venizelos who in 1914 first suggested the idea of a population exchange as a solution to the Greek-

Mindful of Greece's security concern over a revanchist Bulgaria in Macedonia and Turkey's refusal to recognize the status quo in the Aegean, and of the need for time to develop the newly acquired Balkan territories of the past three years,[13] Venizelos recognized the necessity of calming the turbulence in Greek-Turkish relations. Four days later, he accepted, in principle, the Turkish initiative for a voluntary population exchange, provided that the free and spontaneous character of the exchange was secured and that the properties of the emigrants were properly appraised and liquidated. A Mixed Commission for the limited exchange of populations was established in June 1914 at Smyrna [Izmir]. By August the Commission for the valuation and liquidation of the migrants' fixed property started its work by taking dispositions in the Smyrna, Pergamum, and Aydin areas of Asia Minor. But the preliminary work of the Mixed Commission was suspended by the Porte's entry in the World War and the exchange agreement came to naught.[14] In theory at least, the Greek-Turkish agreement of 1914 seemed to suggest that the peaceful exchange of populations as a preventative measure could improve relations between states and solve some of their problems arising out of the presence of significant ethnic and religious minorities. In practice, however, it is highly doubtful that most people would voluntarily leave their ancestral lands and homes for another country, even one of their fellow kinsmen, without being forced to do so or without a powerful incentive. Yet, it is also true that Athens was not adverse to the idea of a population exchange that would help to reinforce the Greek element in the newly acquired territories and would make up for the loss of one-half million Greeks who migrated to the

Turkish problem. Alaeddine Haidar, "Le problèm de l'échange des populations," *Aurore* (Paris) (October 30, 1922); and Calib Kemali Söylemezoğlu, *Hatılarlar [Memoirs]* (Istanbul, 1946), pp. 102–103.

[13]The acquisition of southern Epirus, a large chunk of Macedonia—including the port of Thessaloniki, Crete and the eastern Aegean islands as a result of the Balkan Wars nearly doubled the size of Greek territory and population. Greece's territory increased from 25,014 square miles to 41,933 square miles, and its population rose from 2,666,000 to 4,363,000.

[14]Psomiades, *The Eastern Question*, p. 55; Stephan P. Ladas, *The Exchange of Minorities: Bulgaria, Greece and Turkey* (New York: Macmillan, 1932), pp. 21–22; and Yusuf Hikmet Bayur, *Türk Inkilâbı Tarihi* [History of the Turkish reform], 2:3 (Ankara: Türk Tarih Kurumu Basimevi, 1951), pp. 251–252.

Americas between 1900 and 1914. Its objection was to the poor cor-relation of the peaceful and voluntary emigration of Muslims living in Greek Macedonia and Epiros and the violent and forced exodus of more than 150,000 Greeks from Asia Minor and Eastern Thrace.[15] If the persecutions of the Greek minority then and throughout World War I in Turkey had not occurred, or if the population exchange agreement of 1914 had been peacefully realized, there would have been a major improvement in the direction of Greek-Turkish rela-tions. Undoubtedly, these persecutions were a compelling factor in the subsequent designs of Greece on Greek populated Smyrna and Eastern Thrace.

Finally, following the end of World War I, the Treaty of Neuilly-sur-Seine was signed on November 27, 1919, delimiting Bulgaria's southern frontier and conceding Western Thrace to the Allies for dis-position. On the same day, Greece was assured that autonomy for Western Thrace was out of the question and that the territory would go to Greece.[16] At the same time and place, the Convention for the Reciprocal and Voluntary Emigration of Minorities between Greece and Bulgaria was concluded. And shortly thereafter, Western Thrace, which was occupied by Greek forces during the great autumn Allied Balkan offensive of 1918, was ceded to Greece.

The Convention included the right of ethnic and religious minori-ties to immigrate freely into the territories of their respective moth-erlands; the freedom to take their goods with them; and the loss of one nationality and the immediate acquisition of the other upon their departure. Articles 9–13 provided for a Mixed Commission to supervise and facilitate the voluntary emigration referred to in the Convention, including the evaluation and liquidation of immobile property and disputes over property ownership.[17] On April 17, 1920,

---

[15]*AYE*, 1914: A.A.K. 17. The Greek Minister of Foreign Affairs to the Sublime Porte, Sep-tember 30, 1914.

[16]*Venizelos Papers*, 24, Kanellopoulos (Paris) to the Greek Ministry of Foreign Affairs, November 27, 1919.

[17]For the text of the Convention, see *AYE*, 1922: 105 (2)2,1. For details of its implemen-tation, see Ladas, *The Exchange of Minorities*, Chapter 3; and Dimitri Pentzopoulos, *The Balkan Exchange of Minorities and Its Impact upon Greece* (Paris and the Hague: Mouton, 1962), pp. 67–75.

Venizelos informed the Secretary General of the League of Nations, Sir Eric Drummond, that Greece had ratified the Convention and requested that he place the formation of a Mixed Commission on the agenda of the next meeting of the League Council. Three weeks later, Athens reiterated its wish to the League to put in effect the Convention with Bulgaria as soon as possible.[18] Finally, on November 27, 1920, after much searching, the League Council appointed the two foreign members of the Mixed Commission for the Greek-Bulgarian population exchange, which was also to include one Greek and one Bulgarian. The League's appointees were Lt. Colonel A.C. Corfe of New Zealand and Commandant Marcel de Roover of Belgium. They, along with M. Colban of the League's Secretariat, who also gained much experience in the implementation of the Greek-Bulgarian Convention, were to become valuable members of Dr. Nansen's staff in dealing with the Greek-Turkish refugee question.

The Greek-Bulgarian population exchange was quickened unexpectedly with the sudden influx of thousands of Greek refugees from Eastern Thrace into Western Thrace in October 1922. Unfortunately, the exchange was not without a strong element of coercion, its voluntary character being largely ignored. When only a few from the targeted populations elected to leave voluntarily, both countries began strong agitation to force them out. By 1924, the Greek-Bulgarian population exchange was largely completed. Some 50,000 Greeks, mostly from Bulgaria's Black Sea littoral, were exchanged for about 100,000 Bulgarians, largely from Western Thrace and central and eastern Macedonia, although the questions of properties left behind and compensation were to drag on for several years more.[19] Lastly, the draconian but defunct Treaty of Sèvres of August 10, 1920, also

---

[18]*AYE*, 1920: 53 (2). Caclamanos (London) to Drummond (London), April 17, 1920, and May 8, 1920.

[19]Between 1912 and 1920 alone, over 435,000 refugees in Greece received state assistance, including 200,000 from Thrace and 190,000 from Asia Minor. *AYE*, 1923: 13 (2)2,1. Refugee File. Many had returned to their homes after the end of the world war only to became refugees again less than three years later. The development and experience of a cadre to deal with refugees and population exchanges in the decade prior to its defeat in Asia Minor enabled the Greek government to attend to its 1922–1924 massive refugee problem with far greater efficiency than would normally have been the case.

provided, *inter alia,* for a voluntary and reciprocal exchange of Greek and Turkish populations, as well as the right of refugees to return to their former homes.[20]

## The Setting

The withdrawal of a defeated Greek army from Anatolia in early September 1922,[21] and the Greek loss of Eastern Thrace at the Mudanya armistice talks a month later,[22] decisively shaped the decision that led to the Greek–Turkish population exchange at Lausanne.[23] Those events precipitated a refugee crisis of mammoth proportions and a humanitarian nightmare, dumping on Greece over a million refugees—the vast majority of whom were traumatized and completely destitute.

As the Greek forces retreated to Smyrna, they were accompanied or followed by some 150,000 impoverished and panic-stricken refugees from the interior. In search of security and sustenance, the

---

[20]Psomiades, *The Eastern Question,* pp. 29–30; and Great Britain, Treaty Series no. 12 (1920). *Tripartite Agreement between the British Empire, France and Italy respecting Anatolia . . .* , Cmd 963, London 1920.

[21]The long awaited Turkish offensive began on August 26, 1922, southwest of Afyonkarahisar, at the most vulnerable point on the Greek front. Hopelessly outnumbered, the Greeks were overcome and within a few days the Turks succeeded in cutting the rail link to Smyrna, occupying Afyonkarahisar and totally disrupting the principal Greek route of communications and supplies. Soon, the Greek forces were cut in two and in full retreat. While those in the northern sector, some three divisions, skillfully retreated to the Sea of Marmara and embarked for Greece, the larger concentration of forces, in the southern sector, was completely routed. Disoriented and in disarray, it fled to Smyrna and the coast.

[22]The Mudanya armistice talks, October 3–11, 1922, took place at Mudanya, a small port town on the southern shore of the sea of Marmara. For the Mudanya armistice convention of October 11, 1922, see Appendix I.

[23]Following the armistice of Mudros (October 20, 1918), Greek forces, at the invitation of the Allies, occupied Smyrna (Izmir) in May 1919 and shortly thereafter Eastern Thrace. The long delayed and fateful Near East peace treaty of Sèvres (August 10, 1920), awarded, *inter alia,* to Greece Eastern Thrace and provided for a zone of Greek influence in the Smyrna region that could eventually lead to its annexation by Greece. Among other factors, the Allied occupation of Constantinople in March 1920 and the subsequent onerous Sèvres treaty, allowing for only a truncated Turkey in the middle of Asia Minor with Constantinople as its capital, precipitated a successful Turkish nationalist revival and resistance under Mustapha Kemal [Atatürk]. For a fine treatment of the Greek–Turkish war of 1919–1922, see Michael Llewellyn Smith, *Ionian Vision, Greece in Asia Minor, 1919–1922* (London: A. Lane, 1973).

refugees camped on the city's quay. In an attempt to calm the city's population, the Allied consuls in Smyrna gave formal assurances to the Greeks and Armenians that they need not fear for their lives, although they were not prepared to take concrete steps to ensure the safety of the city's civilian population. Only the American Consul-General, William Horton, refused to give such false assurances and indeed, on September 4, he cabled the US High Commissioner in Constantinople, Admiral Bristol, "in the interest of humanity and for the sake of American interests to mediate with Mustapha Kemal for an amnesty to permit the orderly withdrawal of Greek forces from Anatolia and possibly avoid the destruction of Smyrna."[24] Horton's great concern was who would police the city between the time of the Greek withdrawal and the arrival of the Turkish forces. The response from Washington was simply to send three destroyers to Smyrna for the protection of American lives and property.

On September 8, the Greek army completed its evacuation from Smyrna. The following day, the victorious Turkish forces entered the city and the looting, armed robbery, rape, and killings began. The situation worsened when fire broke out on September 13, and after three days, some two-thirds of Smyrna lay blackened and smoldering. The Armenian, Greek, and European quarters were almost totally destroyed, and those who survived the holocaust were compelled to join the ranks of the refugees on the quay. Without food and water, some 300,000 helpless souls were now so pressed together that "one could not lie down without being crushed to death—women gave birth to stillborn babies and sheltered them against their dried-up breasts, for lack of a burial place . . . waiting for a momentary pathway to open up for them to lay their burdens in the all-receiving sea."[25] In the meantime, the Allied navies (some twenty-one warships—eleven British, five French, two Italian, and three American) congregated in

---

[24]Louis P. Cassimatis, *The American Influence in Greece, 1917–1929* (Kent, OH: Kent State University Press, 1988), p. 111; Marjorie Housepian, *The Smyrna Affair* (New York: Harcourt Brace Jovanovich, 1966), pp. 94–96; and George Horton, *The Blight of Asia* (New York: Bobbs Merrill, 1926).

[25]Melville Chater, "History's Greatest Trek," *The National Geographic Magazine* 48, no. 5 (November 1925): 539.

Smyrna harbor and unashamedly declared their strict neutrality. Their sole mission was to protect the property and lives of their nationals and consuls. None wanted to give even the appearance that they were siding with the Greeks. This encouraged the Turks to believe that whatever action they took against the Ottoman Greeks and Armenians, there would be no interference from the Great Powers.

By September 24, the situation got completely out of hand as Turkish handbills informed the displaced multitude that those not out of the city within a week's time would be deported to the interior.[26] And Nurreddin Pasha, the newly appointed Governor-General of Smyrna, announced that any refugees remaining in the city after September 30 would be massacred.[27] The dramatic result of these announcements was a further stampede of thousands of people toward the harbor, desperately seeking passage to safe haven. Shortly thereafter, given the refusal of Allied ships to provide passage for the refugees and in order to hasten their departure from Turkish soil, the Angora [Ankara] authorities gave the American relief workers in Smyrna assurances that Greek ships could come to Smyrna to take the refugees, provided the ships did not fly the Greek colors and did not dock on the quay. The Athens government at first feared to release its transports, concerned that the Turks would seize them and use them for an invasion of the Greek islands, but it finally relented, and on September 24, Greek rescue vessels flying American colors entered Smyrna harbor. Thus, by October 8, while the armistice talks were taking place at Mudanya, the evacuation of the entire Greek and Armenian population of Smyrna was completed.[28] A week later, the International Red Cross reported that a total of one half-million refugees had reached Greece in wretched condition and that more

---

[26]*Ibid.*, pp. 539–540, and Edward Hale Bierstadt, *The Great Betrayal* (New York: R.M. McBride, 1924), pp. 56–87.

[27]Report of British Foreign Secretary Lord Curzon in *DBFP*, XVIII, Document 48. *British Secretary's Notes of a Conference between French President of the Council, the British Secretary of State for Foreign Affairs, and the Italian Ambassador in Paris, held at the Quai d'Orsay,* September 22, 1922.

[28]Chater, "History's Greatest Trek," pp. 535–540; Smith, *Ionian Vision,* pp. 306–311; Housepian, *Smyrna Affair,* pp. 175–185; and William T. Allis, "Jennings of Smyrna," *Scribner's* (August 1928): 230–235.

were on their way.[29] In the thirty days following the Turkish entry into Smyrna over 50,000 Greek and Armenian civilians lost their lives.[30]

From 1914 to 1917, while Greece was still neutral, over 500,000 Ottoman Greeks were expelled from their homes and deported to the interior, with much loss of life. And in the three years before the Smyrna disaster, the Kemalists continued the policy of the Young Turks with massive deportations, massacres, expropriations, and other assaults on the Christian population. These atrocities were escalated after the failure of the last Greek offensive in Anatolia in September–October 1921 at the Sakarya river. That failure demonstrated to all that Greece could no longer sustain itself in Anatolia.

Consequently, a month later, Greece agreed to place its fate in Asia Minor in the hands of the Allied Powers. After much delay, the three Allied Foreign Ministers met in Paris on March 22, 1922, to arrange for a peace conference. And following five consecutive days of intense negotiations, in which the British and the French were often antagonists, it finally offered its armistice and peace proposals to an anxious Greece and an indifferent Turkey. It called for, *inter allia*, a cessation of hostilities and the peaceful evacuation of Greek forces from Asia Minor in four months. The Greek army would not withdraw until both sides had accepted the preliminary conditions for peace.[31] The

[29] *Nansen Papers*, R 1761 (1922), 48/24380/24357, October 17, 1922.

[30] Harry J. Psomiades, "The American Near East Relief (NER) and the *Megali Catastrophe* in 1922," *Journal of Modern Hellenism* 19 (2001): 137. The American Consul General of Smyrna, George Horton, estimated the figure closer to 100,000. See Housepian, *Smyrna Affair*, pp. 258–259.

[31] The Paris proposals required Greece and Turkey to announce their acceptance not only of the armistice but also their acceptance, in principle, of the Allied peace terms. Only then would they convoke a final peace conference to work out the details. These terms obliged Greece to cede to Turkey a portion of Eastern Thrace providing a sufficient distance from Constantinople to assuage Turkish fears for the security of the city and to withdraw from Smyrna, whose Christian population would be placed under the supervision of the League of Nations, which was to draw up a mechanism for the protection of minorities. Allied troops would be withdrawn from Constantinople after the ratification of the future Treaty of Peace. The Straits would be placed under the supervision of a League of Nations Commission, with a Turkish president. The League of Nations would also seek to obtain a national home in Cilicia for the Armenians. There were also proposals concerning the size of the Turkish armed forces, conscription, and economic, fiscal, and judicial matters with emphasis on the capitulatory system that granted special privileges to foreigners. See Great

beleaguered Greek government immediately accepted the armistice proposals but sought clarification of minority guarantees in the terms for peace. It insisted on firm international guarantees and amnesty for the Greek population of Asia Minor. A decision by Turkey was expected.[32]

On April 5, Turkey announced that it would not accept the armistice without a provision for the immediate evacuation of Greek forces from Anatolia and demanded that the evacuation take place concurrently with the armistice talks and not at the conclusion of a peace treaty.[33] Thus negotiations were stalled and time was on the side of the Turks as they prepared for a final and decisive military victory over the increasingly vulnerable Greek forces.[34] "Turkey is dragging its feet and delays going to the Conference because it knows that the Greeks are at the end of their resources. Therefore they want victory to strengthen their hand."[35]

By the Spring of 1922, the bulk of the Greek population of northern Anatolia (the Pontos), far from the war zone, had been deported into the interior. Along the way, tens of thousands had perished from exposure to the elements, starvation, and disease: typhus, smallpox, dysentery, pneumonia, and influenza were rampant. The dead and half dead were thrown into rivers and ditches.[36] In this region alone,

Britain, *Parliamentary Papers,* Cmd. 1641 (1922). "Pronouncements of the Three Allied Ministers for Foreign Affairs Respecting the Near East Situation, March 17, 1922." Also *DBFP,* XVII, Chapter 4.

[32]Greece's acceptance of the armistice is dated March 25, 1922. *AYE,* 1922: 6 (5)1.

[33]*AYE,* 1922: 6 (5)1. Triantafillakos (Constantinople) to Ministry of Foreign Affairs (Athens), April 5, 1922, and *Ibid:* 88 (2)1,1, April 23, 1922.

[34]At this juncture, the Turkish Nationalists were not interested in making peace with an enemy it believed it could defeat by force of arms; they employed delaying tactics to gain sufficient time for military preparations. They were convinced that with the defeat of Greek forces they could extract better armistice and peace proposals from the Allied Powers. See Osman Okyar, "Turco-British Relations in the Inter-War Period: Fethi Okyar's Mission to London," in William Hale and Ali Ihsan Bagis, editors, *Four Centuries of Turco-British Relations, Studies in Diplomatic, Economic and Cultural Affairs* (North Humberside: Eothen, 1984), pp. 62–79.

[35]*DBFP,* XVII, Doc. 348. Rumbold (Constantinople) to Curzon (London). August 14, 1922.

[36]PRO, FO 331/7876. E 3148/19/44. Turkey. *Memorandum of Mr. Rendel on the Turkish Massacres and Persecutions of Minorities since the Armistice.* March 20, 1922. Written at the request of Lord Curzon by Mr. Rendel of the Eastern Department. For an extensive file on the deportations and death marches see also *AYE* (1923): 18 (5) 1.1. Most of the reports in

between 1914 and 1922, over 300,000 Greeks had perished. The appointments to senior administrative posts at this time, which included Sabit Bey as Vali of Erzerum, Abdul-Halk Bey as Vali of Konia, and Muammer Bey as Mitessarif of Caesarea, told a lot about the temper of the Angora government. All three had been involved in the Armenian genocide. Each had acquired notoriety as a ferocious exponent of the policy of deporting and massacring Christians.[37] Yet, it was not until May 1922 that the Allies, under intense pressure from international public opinion, finally agreed to investigate the "alleged" Turkish atrocities by a Commission of Inquiry. However, not surprisingly, it took considerable time and much haggling among the Allies over the composition of the Commission and the payment of its members before it was finally established.[38] By then it was over-

this file are from eyewitness accounts of American relief workers. They all saw the deportations as a method of extermination. For example, on June 14, 1922, they reported on the deportations that "... many never reach their destination and the method of slow starvation is another method in accomplishing their extermination." For further discussion on the deportations, see also *DBFP*, XVII, Doc. 517. Curzon (Foreign Office) to Lord Hardinge (Paris), February 2, 1922, and Doc. 508. Conversation between Curzon and Pioncaré at the Quai d'Orsay, January 16, 1922, in which they express the belief that "the old Turkish plan of massacre and deportations to get rid of minorities was still in full operation." Even Ankara's ally, the Soviet Union, complained bitterly about the "brutally killed Greeks—old men, children and women." S.I. Aralov, *Vospominaniya Sovietskovo Diplomata, 1922–1923* [Memoirs of a Soviet Diplomat, 1922–1923] (Moscow, 1960), p. 43. Also by the same author "In the Turkey of Atatürk" *International Affairs* [Moscow] 8 (August, 1960): 81–87. Aralov was the Soviet ambassador to Ankara in 1922–1923. See John Nicolopoulos, "The Testimony of Michail Vassilievich Frunze Concerning the Tragedy of Pontic Hellenism," *Journal of Modern Hellenism*, No. 4 (1987): 37–53. Frunze's diary was written in part during his trip to Turkey as ambassador extraordinary of the Soviet Ukranian Republic for the purpose of concluding a treaty with Turkey.

[37] *BFSP*, XVII, Doc. 605. Rumbold (Constantinople) to Curzon (Foreign Office), April 24, 1922. Each was arrested after the armistice, and all three were in due course deported to Malta. From there they made their way to join the Nationalists and were never punished for major atrocities. The list of suspected war criminals who joined the Nationalists and were given high posts in the Ankara government also included Dr. Tevfik Rüstü Aras, later appointed foreign minister, Sükrü Kaya, Mustapha Abdülhalik Renda, Abdulahad Nuri, and Arif Fevzi Pirinççizade. See Taner Akçam, *A Shameful Act: The Armenian Genocide and the Question of Turkish Responsibility* (New York: Metropolitan, 2006), pp. 360–363. Abdulahad Nuri, the brother of Yusuf Kemal Tengirsenk, the foreign minister of the Ankara government in 1921–1922, was briefly held by the Ottoman government as a war criminal in 1920. Tengirsenk sent a warning to Istanbul in the summer of 1922 that if his brother were executed, he would kill at least two or three thousand Armenians. Soon thereafter Nuri was released. *Ibid.*, p. 363.

[38] France. Ministère des Relations Extèrieures, 1919–1929. Levant. *Turquie.* Vol. 56. Series 304–1. *Commission d'enquete en Anatolie et en Thrace, May-Aoüt 1922; and DBFP*, XVII,

taken by events, including the refusal of Angora to admit the Commission to the Pontos or Black Sea region, and it came to naught.[39]

Going through a litany of atrocities is never pleasant. In war, there are always atrocities. But when there is an acknowledged grand system of extermination of a population, such as that in Asia Minor, it has to weigh heavily on the minds of those who must decide the fate of the survivors—the refugees. Another major factor which profoundly influenced the movement toward the population exchange was the armistice of Mudanya, October 3–11, 1922. It set the stage for the Lausanne peace conference and had a direct bearing on the Greek refugee crisis. For the armistice was not simply a matter of a cease-fire and the drawing up of military lines between a defeated Greece and a victorious Turkey but primarily a political settlement reflecting the competing interests and motives of the Great Powers and Turkey. Its reluctant acceptance by Greece and the refusal of the Allies to insist on amnesty for its majority Greek population of 300,000 was to lead immediately to its expected exodus from Eastern Thrace. Mudanya was the last opportunity available to Greece to halt or modify the movement toward a massive population exchange.[40] Moreover, there were serious Greek efforts to undo the Mudanya armistice at Lausanne. If they had been successful, the compulsory exchange agreement would have been cancelled or significantly altered.

At the peak of these tragic events, on September 24, the remnants of the Greek army which had withdrawn to the offshore islands of Chios and Mytilene revolted. Two days later, under the leadership of Colonels Nicholas Plastiras and Stylianos Gonatas, the Revolution reached Athens and the *vouli* or parliament was dissolved. On the following day, September 27, the revolutionaries forced King Constantine to abdicate and assumed authority to govern Greece. The new

Doc. 628. Curzon (London) to Rumbold (Constantinople), May 12, 1922. See also Doc. 633, 649, 673 and 735.

[39]*DBFP,* XVIII. Doc. 45. Sir E. Crowe (Foreign Office) to London (Geneva), September 21, 1922. See also the report of the International Red Cross, *RICR,* Vol. LIII, No. 239, July 15, 1922, p. 617.

[40]Smith, *Ionian Vision,* p. 334. For a detailed study of the Mudanya talks and the events leading up to them, see Harry J. Psomiades, " Eastern Thrace and the Armistice of Mudanya, October 3–11, 1922," *Journal of Modern Hellenism,* 17–18 (Winter 2000–2001): 1–67.

government recognized that its immediate priorities were to attend to the relief of hundreds of thousands of destitute refugees and to reorganize its demoralized military forces into an effective instrument in order to obtain some leverage in the armistice negotiations at Mudanya and the Lausanne peace conference. On the same day, the Revolutionary Government appealed to the League of Nations for refugee assistance and, admitting its own inexperience in foreign policy, called upon Eleftherios Venizelos, the internationally respected statesman and the former prime minister of Greece, who had gone into self-imposed exile in Paris after his disastrous electoral defeat in November 1920, to represent Greece abroad. Venizelos was provided with full powers to deal with foreign policy issues, including the refugee question and the status of the Greek minority in a victorious Kemalist Turkey.[41]

Earlier, on September 19, apprised of the pitiable condition of the Greek refugees, the General Assembly of the League had directed Fridjtof Nansen to utilize the services of his organization (as High Commissioner for Russian refugees) to assist in the relief of Near East refugees, with such resources as the governments of the members of the League of Nations might place at his disposal. Nansen left Geneva for Constantinople on September 30 and arrived there in the first week of October, during the Mudanya armistice talks, expecting to deal with a simple refugee crisis. Instead, he soon found himself playing a leading role in an affair whose scale and implications were far beyond his expectations.

---

[41]For the enormity of the domestic and international issues confronting the Revolutionary Government and for the details of the revolt, see Psomiades, "Eastern Thrace and the Armistice of Mudanya," pp. 12–15.

# PART ONE

# Fridtjof Nansen
# The Special Envoy of the
# League of Nations

# CHAPTER I

# Fridtjof Nansen–From Arctic Explorer to International Civil Servant

## *The Man*

Fritdjof Nansen was born in Christiania (as Oslo was then known) on October 10, 1861. His father was a deeply religious lawyer, and his mother belonged to one of the few aristocratic families in Norway. The family was relatively well off, enabling the young Fridtjof to attend a private school where he excelled in all subjects from classical languages to mathematics and sports. In the 1870s, skiing was rapidly gaining popularity among Christiania's upper class, and was a sport that Nansen mastered and enjoyed throughout his entire life, with great benefit. Nansen's sporting prowess continued to develop; at age 18 he broke the world one-mile skating record, and in the following year, won the national cross-country skiing championship. In 1881, he began his university studies in Christiania and was such a good student of science that in the following year the university sent him on a five-month expedition on the sealer *Viking* to the Arctic to take samples of marine life. It was during this expedition in the waters off Greenland that Nansen first acquired his interest in the polar regions.

Nansen was also a man who thrived on risk and high adventure. While working on his doctorate in zoology in the old Hanseatic town of Bergen, Nansen planned to become the first person to cross Greenland on skis. And in 1888, he realized this ambition and successfully completed in three months the treacherous and grueling journey in the company of three Norwegians and two Sami.[1] It made him an

---

[1]Since no ship was likely to return the party of six to Norway until the following spring, Nansen and his party spent the next seven months in Greenland, hunting, fishing, and studying the life of the local inhabitants. Nansen also put together his notes on the weather and terrain of the previously unexplored interior of Greenland.

instant national hero and an international celebrity.[2] The publication of his book on the Greenland expedition, issued in several languages, also secured Nansen's personal finances. In 1889, he married the singer Eva Sars, who was also an accomplished skier, and settled down to family life and his scholarly pursuits.[3]

But the polar regions were again calling, and the restless Nansen set himself the target of reaching the North Pole by using a ship, designed so as to prevent the ice from pressing it down, which could, according to his revolutionary theory, drift with the ocean currents, crossing the North Pole from east to west. In 1892, he had the polar vessel "Fram" built and a year later allowed the vessel to be frozen into the drift ice north of Siberia in the hope that it would drift over or close to the North Pole. But it soon became manifest that the vessel was drifting too far south. Nansen then left the "Fram" with one crew member—an experienced dog handler, twenty-eight dogs, three sledges, and two kayaks, in March 1895, and set off on a 400-mile dash to the North Pole. They traveled 140 miles over oceans of tumbled ice; and the way ahead was "a veritable chaos of iceblocks stretching as far as the horizon."[4] They got farther north than anyone had been before, but drifting ice and the lack of food compelled them to turn back and seek the mainland. They survived two winters by shooting seals, walruses, and polar bears before making it, miraculously, safely back to Norway in September 1896.[5] Beyond any doubt, Nansen's expeditions to the polar regions not only demonstrated his extraordinary limits of endurance and perseverance but they under-

---

[2]One of the many honors Nansen was to receive from institutions all over Europe was the prestigious *Founder's Medal* of the British Royal Geographical Society.

[3]An enthusiastic adherent of Darwin's new theory of evolution and the notion that all living organisms are related, one of Nansen's projects was to study the nervous system of the hagfish. He believed that such a study would lead to a better understanding of the working of the human central nervous system and brain. His study, *The Structure and Combination of Histological Elements in the Central Nervous System,* published in 1887, led to his doctorate. He is considered as a co-founder of the modern theory of the nervous system or neurology. Nansen also contributed greatly to the new science or discipline of oceanography and may be viewed as one of its founding fathers.

[4]Fridtjof Nansen, *Farthest North,* Vol. II (London: G. Newnes, 1897), pp. 66–67.

[5]Asie Sveen, "Fridtjof Nansen: Scientist and Humanitarian," March 15, 2001, in Nobelprize.org

standably reinforced his belief in his own ability to get things done. He became a man of supreme self confidence. Although he retired from exploration after his return to Norway in 1896, his recorded experiences as explorer, including travel techniques and the use of polar equipment, influenced a generation of subsequent Arctic and Antarctic expeditions.

## The Diplomat

After his return from the Polar ice cap, Nansen once again returned to family life,[6] and to his research, writing, and teaching, including lectures to the scientific communities in London and in several other European capitals.[7] During this period, Nansen also turned his attention to politics and took an active part in the looming crisis between Norway and Sweden that finally in 1905 led to the peaceful dissolution of the union between the two states and Norway's assertion of complete independence.[8] He wrote many articles for the cause, including "The Constitutional Conflict between Norway and Sweden," and applied his considerable influence to advance it. He was largely responsible for persuading Prince Charles of Denmark to accept the throne of a newly independent Norway, who shortly after a referendum was proclaimed king Haakon VII.

Having achieved its independence, a poor and defenseless Norway once again called upon Nansen to exploit his international fame to advance its security interests abroad. The new Norway had based its foreign and defense policy largely on the protection of the British Royal Navy, which controlled its sea lanes. Thus, upon achieving

[6]His daughter Liv was born just before Nansen set out with the "Fram" in 1893. A son was born in 1897, and two daughters in 1900 and 1901, respectively. In the following year, with the profits from his publications, Nansen bought a large and imposing house for his enlarged family. He called it *Polhøgda (Polar Heights)*, and it remained his home for the rest of his life. A fifth and final child was born in 1903, in the new home.

[7]In 1897 Nansen was appointed professor of zoology at the University of Oslo and took on the major task of editing and publishing in six volumes of the scientific results of the "Fram" expedition.

[8]The political union between Norway and Sweden was imposed by the Great Powers in 1814.

independence in the summer of 1905, it soon thereafter appointed Nansen as its first ambassador to Great Britain (1906–1908), with the primary mission of securing a British guarantee for Norway's independence and territorial integrity. In London, the famous Nansen enjoyed a special status, and he soon developed very warm relations with Britain's foreign policy establishment and the city's elite, who were to be of great value to him in future endeavors. He became a friend of Sir Edward Grey, the British Foreign Minister, and a personal friend of the British Royal Family. His mission was not easy because Britain feared that such a treaty would bring on a formal Danish-German understanding. However, with the growing antagonism between London and Berlin and the formation of new European alliances, Britain finally agreed to guarantee Norway's integrity. The treaty was signed on November 2, 1907, and shortly thereafter, with mission accomplished, Nansen resigned his post.[9] After receiving word that his wife was seriously ill, he made his way home to Norway, but before reaching *Polhøgda*, he was informed by telegram that Eva had died.

After a period of mourning, Nansen threw himself into his academic work and had his university professorship re-designated from zoology to oceanography. In 1911, he managed to complete his great two-volume work, *In Northern Mists*, on the history of the explorations of the Arctic region up to the beginning of the sixteenth century. Perhaps it was the completion of that work and his feeling of despondence that led Nansen in 1911 to write his daughter Liv that life was mostly behind him.[10] It was not until 1914, with the outbreak of World War I, that he reappeared in public life.

Once again, Nansen was called upon to use his celebrity status in the service of his country. Norway had declared its neutrality, alongside Denmark and Sweden. As the war progressed, Norway lost much of its overseas trade, which led to an acute shortage of food. Because

[9]After his wife's death, Nansen returned to London. He was persuaded by the Norwegian government to revoke his resignation as ambassador until after the state visit of Britain's King Edward in April 1908.

[10]Liv Nansen Høyer, *Nansen: A Family Portrait*. Translated from the Norwegian by Maurice Michael. (London: Longmans, Green, 1957), p. 190.

Norway was greatly dependent on the importation of American wheat, the situation became critical when the United States entered the war in April 1917 and placed additional restrictions on international trade. To deal with the situation, in June 1917, Nansen was sent to Washington as head of a small delegation to plead Norway's case for food and other supplies. It was a difficult assignment because, in its attempt to maintain its neutrality, Norway had broken the Allied embargo and sold fish to Germany. Moreover, with the war at its peak, the Allies had little patience with neutrals.[11] The negotiations were protracted, but in the end an agreement on food supplies was reached and Nansen returned home.

Nansen was in Washington for about a year, and in that time, he met many Americans, including Herbert Hoover (a future president and the head of the American Relief Administration, whose mission included relief and aid to the victims of war) and President Woodrow Wilson. Thus, Nansen was already a familiar figure to the American delegation at Versailles, when with war's end he appeared in Paris, with the vague idea of doing something for the soon to be created League of Nations, in his capacity as a private citizen and as the representative of Norway's League of Nations Association, of which he was a founding member. Politics at home had precluded him from being a member of the official Norwegian delegation to the peace conference.[12]

## The International Civil Servant

On January 25, 1919, the Paris Peace Conference formally set up a commission to study the creation of the League of Nations, which was high on its agenda. Unfortunately, the establishment of the League was to be an integral part of the German peace treaty and as such remained the prerogative of the victorious Allies. The neutral states were essentially excluded from the discussions for its forma-

---

[11] *Ibid.*, p.191.
[12] On January 17, 1919, Nansen married Sigrun Munthe, a long-time friend. The marriage proved to be an unhappy one and was resented by Nansen's children.

tion, although they were invited to send observers to an unofficial meeting with one of the subcommittees of the commission.

Meanwhile, before and during the negotiations at Versailles, Russia was engulfed in a civil war between the Bolsheviks (or Reds) who had seized power and their opponents the Whites, and at the same time was the object of Allied military intervention—a Polish invasion, the British in the Caucasus, the Americans in Siberia, and the French along with a Greek expeditionary force in the Ukraine. Russian society was on the verge of collapse, and there was the threat of a massive famine. Unable to stem the tide of the Bolshevik onslaught, the Allies, led by the American delegation, came up with the scheme of offering food to Russia if it would stop trying to spread the communist revolution abroad. Food aid was to be used as a means of extracting concessions from Lenin's regime and ameliorating its behavior. To avoid any hint of Allied recognition of the Bolshevik regime and to forestall the objections of the French, Herbert Hoover of the American delegation suggested that it would be best if the Allies appointed a prominent figure from a neutral country to head the entire operation. And as it happened he had someone in mind, "a fine, rugged character, a man of great physical and moral courage—Fridtjof Nansen."[13] In mid-April 1919, as the last Allied troops withdrew from the Ukraine, the Big Four at Versailles approved Hoover's plan of using food as a lever, but it came to naught with the end of the civil war and a Bolshevik victory over the White Russian forces. Moscow saw the plan as Western propaganda, although it found Nansen acceptable and advised its people to be nice to him.

The League of Nations was brought into being at Versailles on June 28, 1919 with the peace treaty with Germany but only became operative on January 10, 1920, when the German treaty came into force. As a new organization, the League had its problems and was yet to establish its own authority, if it were to be more than a debating society. Its field of action was limited by the Great Powers, who made it clear that the institution was essentially created to service their interests, that,

---

[13]Margaret Macmillan, *Paris 1919: Six Months that Changed the World* (New York: Random House, 2002), p. 81; and Huntford, *Nansen*, pp. 483–488.

particularly in political matters, the League should do only those things which they authorized through the Council, and that it should not impose obligations on them. Moreover, the League's ability to act in a timely manner was further restricted by rules that required unanimity on virtually all decisions. Moreover, its authority and prospects for the future were dimmed by the refusal of the United States Senate to ratify membership in the League. Nevertheless, despite these drawbacks, the League of Nations was not without its ardent supporters. Many believed, as Nansen did, that in the League the neutral states by their very nature could play a vital role in the future peaceful world order and could provide for the first time a nonpartisan framework within which truly international action could be taken to meet the challenges of massive human tragedies.

On the morning of November 18, 1920, Nansen attended the first opening of the General Assembly of the League at its new home in Geneva as one of the three Norwegian delegates, a post he actively sought. It was where, until his death in 1930, he was to find an outlet for his exceptional drive and restless spirit in the service of the League's ideals and international humanitarian assistance.

Earlier, in the spring of 1920, more than a year after the Armistice, the Council of the League was compelled to take immediate action to deal with the desperate situation of over 400,000 "forgotten" prisoners of war and interned civilians still held captive in Russia and in central Europe. There was a pressing need to expedite their repatriation. Many of these unfortunate human beings had been held in captivity under appalling conditions, especially in Russia, ever since the first year of the war. The chaotic situation after the end of hostilities was such that neither the International Committee of the Red Cross (ICRC),[14] nor the Allied governments were able to deal with the

---

[14]The International Committee of the Red Cross, essentially wholly a Swiss affair, was founded in 1864 to help soldiers wounded in the battlefield. It experienced unprecedented growth during World War I, especially in locating and assisting prisoners of war. One of its most important new activities was the inspection of the care and facilities provided POW's. The ICRC should not be confused with the International Federation of Red Cross and Red Crescent Societies, nor with the Red Cross national societies, which provide social services and relief in the event of natural and other disasters.

problem effectively, although great efforts were made to do so. The Allies had repatriated their own prisoners and the problem primarily concerned the defeated enemies and Russia. There were many problems to be solved in the repatriation process and many required the cooperation of numerous governments, particularly that of the Soviet Union which the Allied powers refused to recognize.

The League's Secretary General, Sir Eric Drummond, and his immediate staff saw in the situation an opportunity for the League to enhance its reputation and to prove that it was something more than a shell of an organization. Thus, having apprised the League Council of the urgent need to deal with the POW problem, Drummond convinced the Council that this was a mission appropriate for the League. He recommended that it appoint a special commission for prisoners of war with Nansen as its chairman, as he was one of the League's most prominent members and a man uniquely qualified for the task. The chairman had to be someone that all the interested parties had confidence in, was outside of politics, and had the energy and skill to organize such a huge undertaking.

Nansen, at home in Norway, received a telegram from Drummond on behalf of the Council in mid-April 1920, asking if he would take on the assignment as the League's High Commissioner to oversee the repatriation of the POWs to their respective countries. On April 17, 1920, Nansen conveyed his interest in the assignment, and after a meeting with Drummond's emissary, Philip Noel-Baker,[15] agreed to accept the appointment. And thus began Nansen's extraordinary ten-year career as an international civil servant and his singular dedication to international humanitarian assistance until his death.

Nansen immediately understood that his main tasks were to raise the necessary funds and to solve the problem of transport to get the prisoners home before the onslaught of another disastrous winter in

---

[15]Philip Noel-Baker was a member of the British delegation to the peace conference, where he became a great admirer of Nansen and subsequently joined the Secretariat of the League as an advisor to Drummond. It was Baker who recommended Nansen to Drummond to take on the task of repatriation of the POW's. Huntford, *Nansen*, p. 491; and Liv Nansen Høyer, *Nansen*, p. 223.

captivity,[16] while the actual work connected with the registration, care and transportation of the prisoners was left to humanitarian organizations, chiefly the International Committee of the Red Cross (ICRC), the American YMCA, the Swedish Red Cross, and other national Red Cross societies. It was Nansen who introduced branches of the newly created Epidemic Commission of the League to combat the spread of typhus and cholera; he established disinfectant stations where the POWs could be treated before being transferred to their respective homelands. Nansen also had to deal with disputes, often over jurisdiction, between the various relief agencies.

Thanks to his reputation, contacts, and considerable skills as an organizer and negotiator, Nansen persuaded several governments to grant loans to finance the exchange of prisoners. He also persuaded Britain, the main supporter of the League, to release German ships, which were part of war reparations and were interned with their crews, for the repatriation effort. These ships were repaired and equipped at German ports and manned with German crews at a very small cost. Finally, Nansen was successful in cultivating the much needed goodwill of the Soviet authorities. He went to Moscow in July 1920 and won their support after agreeing that he would represent the individual countries which sent him out, and not the League as such,[17] and secured their approval to carry all prisoners of war free of charge on Russian railroads from the interior to various ports. Thus, by the spring of 1921, a total of 154,388 prisoners, representing 25 nationalities, including 12,000 Greek POWs,[18] had been brought out of Russia, while 251,703 were returned to their homes in

[16]The League had furnished Nansen with sufficient funds merely to defray administrative expenses. Nansen took no salary and traveled third class all over Europe in his capacity as High Commissioner of the League.

[17]At that time, the Soviet Union was not a member of the League of Nations.

[18]The League of Nations Archives, *Nansen Papers*, R 1707 (1920), Document 6293. Politis (Athens) to Nansen, August 6, 1920; Nansen to Venizelos (Athens), August 10, 1920; Litvinoff (Moscow) to Nansen, August 18, 1920; and Nansen to Romanos (Geneva), August 26, 1920. These cables also included a plea from Nansen to the Greek government for the repatriation of thousands of destitute Pontic Greeks settlers in the Novorossisk district of south Russia. See also Nikos Petsalis-Diomidis, "Hellenism in Southern Russia and the Ukranian Campaign: Their Effects on the Pontos Question, 1919," *Balkan Studies* 13, no. 2 (1971): 228–229, 250–258.

Russia by the Nansen High Commission. It all was an amazing effort considering that the League had neither funds nor transport at its command for this operation.[19] It was the League's first concrete achievement and gave a much needed boost to its prestige. This success also led Philip Noel-Baker to say, "there is not a country on the continent of Europe where wives and mothers have not wept in gratitude for the work of Nansen."[20]

With this success behind him, Nansen returned to his scientific work in Norway, as well as to his duties with the Norwegian delegation in the General Assembly of the League. By now, as a (if not "the") leading personality of the League, the flamboyant Nansen adopted a recognizable persona, the wearing of a wide-brimmed hat, and engaged in a more active social life, bringing some dash to an otherwise drab Geneva. But Nansen was not allowed to rest upon his laurels. He was soon called upon to take on, almost simultaneously, two critical challenges: a Europe inundated with penurious refugees, mainly Russian, and the great Russian famine.

On February 20, 1921, with the support of the ICRC and with the approval of the League, it was decided that the League should appoint a commission to deal with the crisis situation sparked by the presence of more than one and a half million Russian refugees, scattered throughout Europe, fugitives from the Bolshevik revolution. Repatriation was not favored by the Soviet government, nor by the majority of the refugees. Where could they go? Immigration to the United States and Canada was severely restricted by new quota laws, and Europe was in the grip of the postwar economic depression, with large scale unemployment. Thus, no country was keen to accept them

---

[19]By the summer of 1922, the last of the German and Austrian-Hungarian soldiers who had been in captivity were shipped home across the Baltic. On the return trip, the vessel carried the last Russian prisoners of war from Germany. Altogether about 430,000 POW's were exchanged in less than two years. In his report to the League, Nansen made it clear that most of the work in repatriation was done by the ICRC. For details of this operation, see Clarence Arthur Clausen, *Dr. Fridtjof Nansen's Work as High Commissioner of the League of Nations* (Urbana: University of Illinois, 1932 [thesis abstract]), pp. 4–5; Liv Nansen Høyer, *Nansen*, pp. 223–228; Edward Shackleton, *Nansen the Explorer* (London: H.F. & G. Witherby, 1959), pp. 179–200; and Hunford, *Nansen*, pp. 491–499.

[20]Shackleton, *Nansen the Explorer*, p. 200.

and they remained stateless, in civil and political limbo. The Allied powers were particularly supportive of efforts to deal with the refugee problem, since the defeat of the Whites or the anti-Bolshevik forces brought 131,227 desperate Russian refugees to Allied-occupied Constantinople,[21] a city already hosting over 100,000 destitute Greek and Armenian refugees.

On August 6, 1921, Sir Eric Drummond asked Nansen if he would agree to be the nominee of the League as High Commissioner for Russian Refugees, and he immediately accepted the offer. Nansen's task was to raise the necessary funds, coordinate the relief work of the various private charities, find a home and employment for the refugees, and link his efforts with the ICRC and the International Labour Organization (ILO). While he was not provided with funding from the League, his mandate allowed him free reign to choose his own staff. This advantage was a blessing since he was not compelled to draw from the League's bureaucracy, which by now was laced with much political intrigue and subject to intense pressure by member states to enforce national quotas in League hiring. Undoubtedly, Nansen's many successes were attributed, in part, to his ability to choose able and fully qualified people for his staff, giving short shrift to nepotism and partiality of any kind.

The following month, Nansen set up an office in Constantinople to deal with the Russian refugees: and thus began the long and difficult task of caring for and placing what were essentially political refugees or asylum seekers. By December 1921, he was actively engaged in raising the issue with various European governments.[22]

It did not take long to realize that these stateless refugees had no legal status and were persons without a country who could not legally cross borders. To deal with this problem, Nansen and the ICRC suggested an identity card or document, akin to a passport, which governments would agree to recognize and which became

---

[21] *Revue Internationale de la Croix-Rouge (RICR)*, 3rd Year, No. 22 (January 1, 1921), pp. 44–45.
[22] Jacques Micheli, "Haut commissariat pour les réfugies russes," *RICR*, 4th Year, No. 37, (January 15, 1922), p. 32.

*Proofprint of the "Nansen Passeport" published in France*
*UNHCR/National Library of Norway, Picture Collection*

known as the "Nansen Passeport." The details were worked out by the
Legal Department of the League of Nations, and in July 1922
Nansen's office began issuing the document to the Russian refugees
and later to other refugees who were unable to get ordinary passports. In time, the Nansen passport was honored by fifty-two countries as an official document. Distinguished holders of the much
sought after Nansen passport included the artist Marc Chagall, the
dancer Anna Pavlova, and the composers Sergey Rachmaninoff and
Igor Stravinsky.

With the help of the ICRC and the ILO, Nansen's organization kept
alive thousands of poverty stricken refugees and placed them in the
Slavic countries of southeastern Europe and France. It relieved
Greece of 5,000 needy Russian refugees when that country got its
own vast refugee problem in the autumn of 1922 and lent its support

to thousands of Armenian refugees who were compelled to abandon their homes in Turkey. Nansen also dealt with the problem of 20,000 Russian Jews who were to be driven out of Poland and Romania. He entered into negotiations with these governments, secured a postponement of the decrees of expulsion and with the aid of various Jewish organizations evacuated them safely to other countries. Romania also threatened to expel for military reasons 10,000 non-Jewish refugees, but with the intervention of Nansen, the Romanian government held back and allowed them to settle in its province of Bessarabia, at least until other arrangements could be made.[23] In spite of these successes, the lack of employment or underemployment for the bulk of the refugees remained significant.

Nansen's appointment as the League's High Commissioner for Russian refugees coincided with the call for him to serve as the League's representative to help relieve the suffering caused by the great Russian famine (1921–1923). In the spring of 1921, a severe famine broke out in the Soviet Union, following a widespread failure of crops. Thirty million Russians were threatened with starvation and death. The problem was so acute that Lenin felt obliged to appeal to the West for food aid. Consequently, the ICRC, which normally had jurisdiction in these matters along with other national charities and government organizations, met in conference to take up Lenin's appeal. Nansen attended the conference as the League's representative. The meetings of the conference were contentious and dragged on for some time, given the distrust of Lenin and the uncompromising anti-Bolshevik position of the politicians, who reintroduced the idea of using food aid as a political weapon. They argued that the famine was not the result of bad weather but was caused by evil rulers, that the Soviet system itself was the root cause of the famine. There was the fear that food aid would only strengthen the despised Bolshevik regime. In response, Nansen and most of the humanitarian organizations argued that they could not stand aside while millions of human beings were threatened with starvation and death;

---

[23]Clausen, *Dr. Fridtjof Nansen's Work*, pp. 7–9.

and that, in this critical situation, humanitarian intervention should not be subordinate to political considerations.[24]

When Nansen agreed to take on the position as the League's High Commissioner for Russian refugees, he also agreed to accept the appointment of the ICRC, as the League's nominee, as the High Commissioner for Russian Relief Famine. On August 27, 1921, he signed an agreement with the Russian government on famine relief. His plate now was overloaded, and many would argue that to take on both assignments simultaneously was a great miscalculation on the part of Nansen and the League's secretariat. Unlike his work with the Russian refugees, Nansen had to endure much opposition from the Great Powers in the Council of the League, who voiced the opinion that Nansen was naive and that he had no idea that he was being used by Lenin for ulterior political purposes. Despite Nansen's eloquent and desperate pleas for assistance, they refused to lend their support. Thus, Nansen had to rely largely on private organizations and his own fund-raising to combat the famine.

Meanwhile, acting independently of the Europeans and the ICRC, the United States took on the bulk of the work of famine relief. In response to the Soviet appeal for aid in the spring of 1921, the American Relief Administration, a highly organized and efficient organization, headed by Herbert Hoover, negotiated an agreement with the Russians. In return for the food aid, the Russians would release all of the remaining American prisoners and use their gold reserves to buy grain from the United States. By the time the famine had largely come to an end in the autumn of 1922, over one million Russians had perished for the lack of food. But millions were saved. The Hoover organization kept over eight and a half million people from starving to death.[25]

At the time that Nansen set up an office for the Russian Refugees in Constantinople in September 1921, he also opened a Nansen Office in Berlin to support and coordinate the work of the European

[24]Liv Nansen Høyer, *Nansen*, pp. 228–237; Huntford, *Nansen*, pp. 500–514; and Shackleton, *Nansen the Explorer*, pp. 200–204.
[25]Huntford, *Nansen*, p. 511.

charities for the Russian famine relief. However, without the support of the major European powers, his efforts met with limited success. He and the private organizations operated for about a year, at the height of the famine, and brought succor to close to half a million inhabitants of the Soviet Union.[26]

Thus, in a very short period of time, Nansen had managed to shape the League as an instrument by which international action could be taken to meet the challenges of massive disasters, made by either man or nature. But more was to come. On September 19, 1922, the day before his commission for Russian famine relief came to an end, Nansen, as High Commissioner for refugees, was once more called upon to play a central role in another major tragedy—a role for which he was exceptionally qualified to play. It was to be his most serious challenge as an intellectual, a statesman, and an international civil servant.

[26]For details of Nansen's work with the Russian famine see: *RICR,* 3rd Year, No. 33 (September 15, 1921), pp. 899–918; and *RICR,* 4th Year, No. 42 (June 15, 1922), pp. 469–481, 794–801, and 899–818.

# CHAPTER II

# The Nansen Initiative for Near East Refugee Relief

On September 16, 1922, after the defeat of Greek arms and the carnage of Smyrna (Izmir), which heralded the mass exodus of the Greek Christian population from Anatolia, Nansen received an urgent request from Lt. Colonel Procter, his deputy High Commissioner for Russian Refugees in Allied-held Constantinople. The telegram read: "Situation of Anatolian Refugees is extremely serious; around 130,000 from the Smyrna region and 70,000 from the Brouse Region. Famine imminent. Propose that the League offer the services of its local organization in Constantinople to administer some funds from Britain and other countries."[1] The request was not unexpected. Nansen had been following events in the Near East very closely and apparently was waiting for the opportunity to get involved, not only in administering relief but politically as well.[2] It was on the very day of Procter's cable that the British government issued the so-called manifest of September 16, calling for the defense of "the deep water line between Europe and Asia against a violent and hostile Turkish aggression." It looked as if Britain were drifting toward another war in the Near East.[3]

---

[1] *Nansen Papers*, R603 (1922),11/23534/22490, September 16, 1922; and Étienne Clouzot, "La Société des Nations et les secours dans le Proche Orient," *RICR*, 4th Year, No. 47 (November, 1922), pp. 972–979.

[2] At the first Assembly of the League in 1920, as the delegate from Norway, Nansen suggested that 60,000 soldiers be sent at once to the Near East to save the Armenians from the onslaught of the Kemalists. He also broached the issue at the Second and Third Assemblies of the League, 1921 and 1922, respectively. See E. E. Reynolds, *Nansen* (Harmondsworth: Penguin, 1949), p. 253.

[3] On September 19, the British softened their attitude for the sake of Allied unity, and after a long and acrimonious dispute at the Quay d'Orsay, the three Allied foreign ministers issued the Allied Note of September 23, 1922, calling for an armistice between Greece and Turkey followed by a peace conference. Nevertheless, as the days passed it looked as if Britain would once again find itself at war. Turkish forces had entered the Neutral Zone of the

It is in the midst of this turmoil that Nansen, in his capacity as a Norwegian delegate to the General Assembly of the League, immediately informed his government of Procter's urgent request and asked for its permission not only to present the request to the League but also to add to it an appeal to Article 11 of the Covenant of the League of Nations, empowering him to offer the good offices of his organization to work toward the immediate end of hostilities between the belligerents of the Greek-Turkish war. And on the same day, September 16, Nansen endorsed and transmitted Procter's request to the President of the Third Assembly of the League and added his proposal that his good offices be offered to the belligerents to stop the war.[4]

The matter was directed to the Fifth Committee of the General Assembly, which dealt with all projects involving funding. Due to the critical nature of Nansen's request and to certain parliamentary maneuvers, it was promptly considered. To ensure its passage, Nansen recommended in the discussions that the intervention of the League take place under the following conditions: (1) Nansen's organization would be charged with the administration of funds raised from other sources and not from the League's regular budget; (2) the work with Russian refugees would continue unhindered; (3) it should be well understood that the League does not assume responsibility for the refugees of Asia Minor; and (4) the intervention of the League would be of a temporary character and would begin at once.[5]

On September 18, the Fifth Committee passed a resolution recommending, in accordance with Nansen's proposals, that the organ-

---

Straits, creating a militarily dangerous and politically delicate situation. By the 27th, Turkish troops had advanced against the British lines at Chanak. London was prepared to issue an ultimatum: "if you do not withdraw from the Neutral Zone around Chanak, you will be fired upon." It was not until October 1 that a war at Chanak was averted. The ultimatum was not delivered, and the Nationalists finally responded to the Allied note of September 23 and agreed to send delegates to the proposed armistice talks at Mudanya. Psomiades, "Eastern Thrace and the Armistice of Mudanya," pp. 2–12.

[4]*Nansen Papers,* R 1761 (1922), 11/23534/12, President of the League Assembly to Nansen, Fourth Session, September 16, 1922.

[5]Clouzot, "La Société des Nations et les secours dans le Proche Orient," p. 972.

ization of the Assistant Commissioner for Russian Refugees in Constantinople should be utilized to administer relief to the refugees of Asia Minor and that in accordance with Article 11 of the Covenant, the Council of the League should consider the feasability of offering good offices to the belligerents with a view to immediate cessation of hostilities.[6] On the next day, in a plenary meeting of the League Assembly, the recommendation of the Fifth Committee was accepted, and a resolution was adopted authorizing the utilization of the Russian refugee organization for the relief of the Asia Minor refugees in Constantinople. It further charged the High Commissioner for Refugees with the duty of investigating the problem raised by the evacuation of a great number of refugees from Asia Minor as a result of military operations, and with the task of bringing relief to those refugees. He was also to assist the authorities of the belligerent countries in a policy of reconstruction with such resources as the Governments of the members of the League might place at his disposal.[7] Given its vulnerable and isolated position at the Turkish Straits and the looming threat of war, the British government actively sought approval of the resolution, welcoming the help of the League of Nations in securing a peaceful settlement in the Near East.[8]

The funds at Nansen's disposal were by no means sufficient to cope with the problem of refugee relief. Member states of the League who were asked to make a contribution were slow to respond. Luckily, on September 25, prior to Nansen's scheduled departure for Constantinople, Lord Balfour, delegate of the British Empire to the General Assembly, announced a major contribution in support of the Nansen organization, with the caveat that it be matched. He told the Assem-

---

[6]League of Nations, Greek and Armenian Refugees from Asia Minor in Constantinople. Resolution adopted by the Fifth Committee on September 18, 1922. A,80 (1922), Geneva.

[7]*Nansen Papers*, R. 1761 (1922), 48/24400/24537. "Memorandum of the High Commissioner of the League of Nations for Refugees," October 10, 1922; *LNOJ* (November , 1922), pp. 1140–1141, 1195–1196; and League of Nations, *Records of the Third Assembly*, Plenary meetings, pp.123–125, 137–142. The machinery which had been established to deal with the Russian refugees had earlier been extended to include over 600,000 Armenians who had survived the war-time massacres in Turkey and had fled to the neighboring states and Europe, making many of them eligible for Nansen passports.

[8]*DBFP*, XVIII, Doc. 45, Crowe (Foreign Office)) to London (Geneva), September 21, 1922.

bly that he had been informed by his government of the real danger of a veritable calamity for the large number of Armenians and Greeks without food and shelter and that his government would make a contribution of £50,000, on condition that it is collectively matched by the other members of the League. Nansen got only £19,208 from ten members, and Britain added a like amount.[9]

Still, three days after Balfour's pledge, Nansen moved swiftly and directed the purchase of 1,400 crates of clothing, 500 tons of wheat from Egypt, and later 1,000 tons of wheat from Bulgaria for distribution to the refugees who had fled from Anatolia to the Greek islands of Samos and Chios, to Constantinople, and to Eastern Thrace. He also ordered that 200 tons of wheat be given to the ICRC for Turkish refugees in Anatolia.[10]

On September 27, 1922, from his headquarters in Geneva, Nansen telegraphed Mustapha Kemal (Atatürk), head of the Revolutionary Government in Angora (Ankara), expressing his earnest desire to enter into relations with his government with respect to the questions of relief entrusted to him. For good measure, the chief of the Persian (Iranian) delegation of the League Assembly also telegraphed Angora, at Nansen's request, drawing the attention of the Nationalist government to the importance of Nansen's mission.[11] At the same time, appalled at the immensity of a potential disaster as 600,000

[9]League of Nations, *General Assembly.* Doc. C736(a); C.100, M.40(1923); C.347 (1923); and A.30 (1923). Clouzot, "La Société des Nations et les secours dans le Proche Orient," p. 974.

[10]The ICRC and the International Union for Aid Relief to Children also responded to the news of the Asia Minor disaster by sending out a mission for relief work. It arrived in Constantinople, by way of the Orient Express, on September 25, and left immediately for Anatolia. Rodolphe Haccius and Henri Cuénod, "Mission en Anatolie," *RICR*, 4th Year, No. 47 (November 1922), pp. 961–971. At the same time, an ICRC delegate arrived in Athens to help organize relief for the first wave of Greek refugees debarking from Smyrna. Rodolphe de Reding-Biberegg, "Secours aux réfugiés grecs," *RICR*, 4th Year, No. 47 (November 1922), pp. 951–960.

[11]*Nansen Papers,* R 1761 (1922), 48/24318/24318, "Report of Dr. Nansen to the League Council, Part I," November 15, 1922. Turkey was not a member of the League, which could possibly create problems for the Nansen mission. On the other hand, although the Soviet Union was not a member of the League, and in fact antagonistic toward it, Nansen was able to deal effectively with Moscow in carrying out his mission as High Commissioner of the League for the exchange of prisoners of war. Persia was the leading Islamic state member of the League and as such it was thought that Persia's endorsement would be helpful to Nansen.

hungry and homeless refugees, mostly women and children, and more to come, swamped Greece, the interim Revolutionary Government, which had just installed itself in Athens, sent SOS telegrams to relief organizations abroad for refugee assistance and one directly to Nansen in Geneva. Further help on a significant scale was absolutely imperative if a great catastrophe was to be averted.

On September 30, Nansen, accompanied by his assistant Noel-Baker, left Geneva for Constantinople, arriving there on October 5. When he arrived in the former Ottoman capital, the armistice negotiations at Mudanya were taking place, and there was still the distinct possibility of the renewal of hostilities.[12] In this crisis atmosphere, Nansen immediately entered into negotiations with his representatives in Constantinople, as well as with the foreign relief organizations based in that city. After several meetings, it became abundantly clear to him that the situation of the refugees was extremely grave, that Turkey would not accept the return of the refugees to their homes, and that the question of their ultimate absorption and settlement was therefore of the utmost importance.[13] These thoughts were reinforced by his conversations with the Allied High Commissioners in Constantinople, who kept him informed of the developments at the Mudanya armistice talks. At the conclusion of those talks on October 11, Nansen again met with the Allied High Commissioners, who reiterated their support for his efforts on behalf of the refugees and asked him to deal with the exchange of prisoners, now that an armistice of the Greek-Turkish war was concluded.[14] At the same time, he presided over an emergency meeting of the representatives of all the international aid organizations, to coordinate their relief activities, to discuss the availability of resources, and to exchange information on the location and status of the refugees.[15] This was a

[12]Psomiades, "Eastern Thrace and the Armistice of Mudanya," pp. 15–33.

[13]For the minutes of the meetings see *Nansen Papers*, R 1761 (1922), 48/24385/24357. October 4 and 6, 1922.

[14]Clouzot, "La Société des Nations et les secours dans le Proche Orient," p. 976.

[15]Nansen was unable to carry through with his intentions to journey to Asia Minor, and had to rely for most of his information concerning the situation there on official reports of the Allied High Commissioners, the Greek government, the Ecumenical Patriarchate, foreign relief workers on the spot as well as those of the representatives of the refugees. *Nansen*

critical moment because at both meetings all were in agreement that the situation would worsen with the implementation of the Mudanya agreements of October 11 and with the anticipated massive flight of the Christian population from Eastern Thrace, which would add another 250,000 refugees to the 750,000 that fled to Greece.[16] Thus, immediately following these meetings, Nansen informed the Secretary General of the League that he considered the refugee problem "far more serious even than that presented to the Assembly" and asked for a global fund-raising campaign to support a massive relief effort.[17]

On October 15, 1922, at the urging of the British government, the Council of the League decided to give the Nansen organization 100,000 Swiss francs and a promise of further funding. Clearly, the funds were in response to the anticipated massive exodus of the Christian population of Eastern Thrace and the need to set up some kind of an organization "to act as liaison between the Greek and Turkish authorities to ensure a gradual and orderly evacuation and to examine the whole question of transfer of population." The assignment was given to Nansen, on behalf of the League, with the understanding that the role of the Allied High Commissioners would be limited as far as possible, using their good offices if necessary.[18] The directive came rather late, as tens of thousands of panic-stricken Christians, upon hearing that the Turks were coming and ever mindful of the massacre of the Greeks in Anatolia, immediately abandoned their homes, crops, and fields and fled to Greece. Indeed, as soon as they saw the Greek troops striking camp, within hours hundreds of villages were deserted. On October 19, Nansen witnessed

---

Papers, "Refugees in Greece and Asia Minor," R1761 (1922), 48/24722/24357. November 18, 1922.

   [16]Briefly, the armistice of Mudanya called for, *inter alia*, the withdrawal of the Greek army from Eastern Thrace in 15 days, and the retro cession of Eastern Thrace to the Turkish administration in 30 days thereafter. Despite the strong objections of Greece, it did not provide for amnesty and security guarantees for the Christian population. The Armistice provisions were to be operative on October 15, 1922. For the Mudanya convention see Appendix I.

   [17]*LNOJ*, 3rd Year, No. 11 (November 1922), p. 1141.

   [18]*DBFP*, XVII, Doc. 26. Rumbold (Constantinople) to Curzon( London), October 16, 1922; and Clouzot, "La Société des Nations et les secours dans le Proche Orient," p. 975.

these events as he traveled by automobile through Eastern Thrace from Constantinople to the Evros (Maritsa) river and onward into Greek territory.

The funds at Nansen's disposal were completely inadequate to cope with the demands of a massive refugee relief program. Fortunately, much of the burden was also carried by the immense efforts of the Greek government and of Greek civil society, by American philanthropy,[19] as well as by other international relief organizations.[20] Yet, the sad fact is that between September 1922 and July 1923, some 70,000 Greek refugees died of malnutrition and disease.[21]

However, even with limited financial resources, Nansen was able to bring direct relief to tens of thousands of refugees.[22] He sent prodigious quantities of food and clothing, arranging for ships to trans-

[19]*Nansen Papers,* R 1761(1922), 48/2477/24357, "Nansen's Report: Refugees in Greece and Asia Minor," Part II, (Geneva), November 18, 1922; Cassimatis, *American Influence in Greece,* pp. 110–117; Dimitra M. Giannuli, *American Philanthropy in the Near East: Relief to the Ottoman Greek Refugees, 1922–1923* (Ph.D. Dissertation, Kent State University, 1992); and Areti Tounda-Fergadi, "L'histoire de l'emprunt accorde pour les réfugiés de 1924," *Balkan Studies* 24, no. 1 (1983): 90–91.

[20]The American Red Cross fed and cared for over 700,000 refugees in Greece from October 1922 to April 1923. The American Women's Hospital organized 33 medical stations ands hospitals. Also active in the Greek relief effort were the YMCA and the YWCA, the American Foreign Missions Board, the Anglo-American Committee of Thessaloniki, and the Athens American Relief Committee. In addition to governments, the Greek Red Cross and private Greek initiatives, the European relief committees at work in Greece from October 1922 to June 1923 included the British Red Cross, the British Relief Committee, Save the Children's Fund (UK), which contributed over 50,000 rations to children and adults, and others, including Swiss, Swedish, and Dutch groups in Athens. For more details see Rodolphe de Reding-Biberegg, "Secours aux réfugiés grecs," pp. 951–960; Apostolos Doxiades, "La situation des réfugiés en Grèce," *RICR,* 6th Year, No. 47, August 1924, pp. 724–734; and Louis P. Cassimatis, *American Influence in Greece,* pp. 117–119, 126–134. For the extraordinary work of the American Near East Relief (NER), which was responsible for most of the relief work in Asia Minor, see Harry J Psomiades, "The American Near East Relief (NER) and the *Megali Catastrophe* in 1922."

[21]*LNOJ,* 4*th* Year, No. 8 (August 1923), Annex 534, p. 644.

[22]For the details of the relief work of Nansen's organization, see his successive reports to the League in *League of Nations Archives,* C.736 (a), M. 447 (a), 1922; C.100, M.40, 1923; C.347, 1923; and A.30. 1923, XII. Although Nansen's High Commission was instrumental in restoring 10,000 Muslim refugees to their homes along the west coast of Anatolia and in caring for and repatriating some 60,000 Muslim refugees in the vicinity of Constantinople, it was mutually agreed that the Angora government, aided by the Red Crescent would be able to cope successfully with matters in Asia Minor without further aid from the League. See also Clausen, *Dr. Fridtjof Nansen's Work,* pp. 9–11; and Clouzot, "La Société des Nations et les secours dans le Proche Orient," pp. 967–977.

port them, to the Greek islands off the Anatolian coast, to Constantinople, and to Thrace. His numerous aides were also actively involved in relief work on mainland Greece, particularly in Athens and Thessaloniki. He planned, organized and funded settlements for 15,000 refugees in Western Thrace. The success of these settlements prompted the International Refugee Resettlement Commission, established in Greece in 1924, to adopt them as models for the installation of similar settlements throughout northern Greece.[23]

Nansen's base of operations was in Allied-held Constantinople, which was the first stop on the way to Greece for tens of thousands of refugees, mainly Greeks from the Pontos or Black Sea region of Anatolia. These wretched souls were held in holding camps, in conditions unfit even for animals. In these camps, especially those in the notorious Selimyeh Barracks, between 30 and 300 refugees died daily from typhus, cholera or smallpox. One observer described the camps as "a veritable morgue."[24]

To respond to this appalling situation, Nansen called in the League of Nations' Epidemic Commission to deal with the various epidemics which were rife throughout the camps; and to instal disinfectant stations not only in Constantinople but also along the banks of the Evros river, where refugees could be treated before continuing on to Greece. As an example of this work, in January-February 1923, 27,000 refugees arrived in Constantinople from the Pontos, but the Greek government refused to accept them since many of them were infected with typhus and smallpox. Nansen took charge of them,

---

[23]*LNOJ,* 5th Year, No. 4 (April 1924). Annex 610, No. C. 91. M. 30. 1924, II, p. 586.

[24]The death toll at the Black Sea ports of Samsun, Ordu, and Trebizond (Trabzon) was also extremely high. Expelled from their homes and left without food, clothing, and medical assistance, death overtook thousands of Greeks, at the Black Sea ports, on board the tossing rescue ships, and in the camps at Constantinople. *The Daily Telegraph* (London) (October 10, 1922); *Nansen Papers,* R 1761 (1922), 48/149382/4938, Childs (Constantinople) to High Commission for Refugees (Geneva), October 19, 1923; and *AYE* (1922), AAK (13), *Pontos.* Fermanoğlu (Constantinople) to the Greek Ministry of Foreign Affairs, October 31, 1922. Without the activities of the American Near East Relief in the Pontos (the League of Nations was prohibited by the Nationalists from operating in the region) and its work jointly with Nansen's organization in Constantinople, "an additional 100,000 refugees would undoubtedly have perished of hunger and disease." *American Near East Relief Activities in Greece,* September 1922 to December 1924, p. 1.

provided them with food and clothing, and made arrangements to have them thoroughly disinfected and placed in clean camps. All told, the League's High Commissioner for Refugees was instrumental in the safe evacuation of over 156,000 Greek refugees from Constantinople.[25]

In Alexandroupolis (Dedeagatch), he set up a fifty-bed hospital to treat and disinfect the refugees flowing across the border from Eastern Thrace. Nansen also placed epidemic teams in Greece, where typhus engulfed all the ports and most of the towns and cities.[26] Finally, thanks to his celebrity status, Nansen's success in his demarche with governments and in his solicitation of world public opinion on behalf of the refugees reinforced the notion that the refugee problem was an international responsibility. But Nansen's work did not cease with his significant contribution to Greek refugee relief. He was soon to confront another challenge, in which his intellectual acumen, diplomatic skills and humanitarian instincts were to serve him well; namely, the challenge in reaching an over-all settlement of the refugee question and of other vital issues related to the cession of Greek-Turkish hostilities.

## The Exchange of Prisoners of War and Civilian Hostages

From his previous experience with refugees, Nansen realized that there was a limit on how long refugees could be fed and clothed by charitable and governmental organizations. Moreover, prolonged charity, he believed, would only demoralize the refugees. Thus, almost from the moment he arrived in Constantinople, his mind turned toward how to make the Near East refugees self-reliant and self-sufficient, without prejudging the final political solution to the refugee problem. Before long, Nansen and his collaborators, Colonels Procter and Trevlar, began an experiment to establish rural Anatolian refugees on vacant land in Western Thrace.[27] It soon became clear, however,

---

[25]Clausen, *Dr. Fridtjof Nansen's Work*, p. 10.
[26]*RICR*, 6th Year, No. 264 (August, 1924), p. 727.
[27]*Nansen Papers*, C 1767 (1922), 48/40233/38170, September 29, 1923. Within nine

that the success of this plan on a larger scale would depend upon the release of thousands of the male hostages detained in Asia Minor by the Turks. In a meeting on October 6 with Rumbold, the British High Commissioner in Constantinople, Nansen spoke of his plan to help make the refugees self-sufficient and of the need to obtain the immediate release of the hostages. Ankara had detained nearly all of the Greek males of Anatolia, ages 17–45, while their families left for Greece, and placed them in the notorious military labor battalions. It was agreed that the release by Turkey of these 100,000 hostages of military age should be given high priority and that their absence greatly complicated the problem of relief and refugee resettlement.[28] Seventy-five percent of the refugees were women, children and the elderly. Deprived of their natural protectors and bread earners, they were exposed to all sorts of physical and moral dangers. On October 10, Nansen conveyed these thoughts at a meeting with all of the Allied High Commissioners and the Principal Allied Powers, along with a guarantee by the League that if the hostages were released, they would not be conscripted into the Greek army. At the same time, to prevent the mass exodus of the Greek population of Eastern Thrace, he made a forceful but unsuccessful effort to persuade the Allied High Commissioners to insert in the Mudanya armistice convention a provision for the immediate release of the Greek civilian hostages by the Nationalist government.[29] The failure of the Allied Powers to follow up at Mudanya, on Nansen's request, beyond question contributed to the flight of the Greek population from Eastern Thrace.

Nansen's next move, also on October 10, was to convey to the Greek government his thoughts and recommendations concerning the settlement of the refugees and also of the urgent need to effect an exchange of the Greek men of military age, detained by the Turks, for

---

months some 15,000 refugees were established in a model colony of 15 villages. They wished to demonstrate that if the refugees were supplied with fields to cultivate they could become self-supporting. *LNOJ,* 4th Year, No. 6 (June 1923), Annex 515, "Near East Refugees: Western Thrace Refugee Settlement," No. C.347. 1923, pp. 696–703.

[28] *DBFP,* XVIII, Doc. 202, Rendal (Eastern Department of the Foreign Office) to Curzon (Foreign Office), November 17, 1922.

[29] *Nansen Papers,* R 1709 (1922), 42/24292//24034, October 10, 1922.

the Turkish nationals held by the Greeks.[30] In his special report to the League on Near Eastern refugees, Nansen clearly admitted in his letter to Venizelos that he tried to promote an exchange of detained Greek hostages in Asia Minor in order to induce the Greek government to accept his plan for the settlement of the Asia Minor refugees on the unoccupied lands of northern Greece.[31] Clearly, his plan not only embraced simple humanitarian concerns but also suggested a solution for the refugees' future fate. By this time, Nansen was convinced that most of the Anatolian refugees would not be permitted to return to their homes and that their welfare demanded that they should be resettled elsewhere as soon as possible. In any case, he believed that either the Greek government would be compelled to contemplate implementing an exchange of population agreement with Turkey in order to make Muslim homes and lands available to the Christian refugees, or, barring such an agreement, it would be forced to settle the refugees on the free lands of Macedonia and Western Thrace.[32] While Nansen was not directly advocating a proposal for a population exchange between Greece and Turkey (that was to come later in his letter of October 10, 1922), he expressed a vague preference for such an exchange.[33]

The consequences of the Mudanya armistice convention of October 11, 1922, prompted the Allied governments to seek arrangements for the exchange of prisoners of war and of civilian hostages and compelled them to participate in a solution to the Greek refugee problem. By now the number of destitute and disease-ridden refugees in Constantinople had increased considerably and posed a

---

[30] *Venizelos Papers,* 318, Nansen (Constantinople) to Venizelos (London), October 10, 1922; *Nansen Papers,* R1761 (1922), 48/24318/24318, Nansen to Venizelos, October 10, 1922.

[31] *Nansen Papers,* R 1761 (1922), 48/24373/24375. SR.I, October 25, 1922.

[32] *Ibid.*

[33] Constantine Svolopoulos, *I apofasi gia tin ypohreotiki andalagi ton plithismon metaxi Ellados kai Tourkias* [The decision for the compulsory exchange of population between Greece and Turkey] (Thessaloniki: Etairia Makedonikon Spoudon, 1981), pp. 10–12. The discussions for an exchange of populations between Greece and Turkey, immediately prior to the Lausanne peace conference, will be dealt with in detail in chapter III of this study. They appear very briefly in this chapter because they are often taken up in the same documents concerning the exchange of prisoners of war and civilian hostages, with which they are interrelated.

major threat to the health of the Allied occupation forces in that city. And their presence prodded the moral sense of the Allied authorities, reminding them of their share of responsibility for the refugees' woes. Small wonder that they were soon to welcome Nansen's efforts to deal with the refugees and related issues, and to assure him of their complete support and cooperation. Moreover, the massive flow of destitute refugees into an impoverished, war weary Greece, unable to care for them without considerable assistance from abroad, posed a potent threat to the peace of Europe. The danger of a political and humanitarian crisis of colossal proportions had to be contained. There was a very real possibility of the disintegration of Greek society and the collapse of its governing institutions.

On October 12, in an urgent note to the Allied High Commissioners, Nansen made essentially the same proposal to them as he had to Venizelos in his letter of October 10. He pleaded that all hopes for a settlement of the refugee problem and for the reconstruction of Greece depended on securing the immediate release of the detained male refugees in Turkey. Failure to secure their freedom, he told them, would create such turmoil in Greece as to invite the triumph of Bolshevism in that country. Moreover, he charged that unless the detainees were united with their families soon, they would be killed off in the Turkish labor battalions, in which tens of thousands of Armenians and Greeks had died of maltreatment during the war. He warned them that mortality in the work gangs was incomparably higher than at the front and that conditions would worsen for them with the onset of winter. (The life-span of a Greek or Armenian in a Turkish labor battalion was generally about two months.)[34] He informed the Allies that should they support his request for the release of the hostages, he would raise the issue officially with the Greek government and attempt to secure its approval for the release of the hostages on an exchange basis.[35] Nansen also informed the

[34]Great Britain, FO 371/7960, E11885/10524/44, *Memorandum by Mr. Rendel on Turkish Atrocities between March to October 1922, October 30, 1922.*

[35]*Nansen Papers*, R 1709 (1922), 42/24356/24034. "Note to the Allied High Commissioners on the Retention of Male Refugees in Asia Minor," October 12, 1922.

Allied High Commissioners shortly thereafter of the Venizelos telegram of October 13, requesting that he, in his capacity as the League's High Commissioner for Refugees, endeavor to arrange for an immediate exchange of Greek and Turkish populations in order to provide some of the refugees in Greece with the housing and accommodations of the departing Muslims. Venizelos made this request because of pronouncements from Angora that the Nationalists would not allow the further presence of Greeks on Turkish soil.[36]

Anxious to move as quickly as possible on the unsettled conditions in Greece and Turkey, the Allied High Commissioners on October 15, on the day the Mudanya convention came into force, extended to Nansen a formal invitation, on behalf of their governments, to deal with the population exchange and with the problem of the prisoners of war and the civilian hostages in his capacity as the League's High Commissioner for Refugees and for Prisoners of War. More specifically, they requested that Nansen endeavor to arrange for the establishment under his presidency of a joint Greek-Turkish Commission to examine the possibility of an immediate exchange of prisoners of war and civilian hostages. They asked that he undertake these tasks as soon as possible and independently of peace negotiations. Not unexpectedly, Nansen promptly accepted the invitation, informed the League of these developments, and initiated a new round of talks with Athens and Angora.[37]

Two days later, on October 17, Nansen received Venizelos' second telegram, in which he expressed his complete agreement with Nansen on the subject of an exchange of civilian populations and on the exchange of prisoners of war and civilian hostages. He informed Nansen that he had asked the Greek government to give him its full support. He warned, however, that on the question of the release of

---

[36] *Nansen Papers*, R 1761 (1922), 48/24318/24318, Venizelos (London) to Nansen (Constantinople), October 13, 1922.

[37] *Nansen Papers*, R 1761 (1922), 48/24929/24357. October 15, 1922. Yet earlier, on October 2, Pioncaré, president and foreign minister of France, told the Greek minister in Paris, Romanos, that the powers would do nothing for the thousands of Greek POW's held in Turkey. *Venizelos Papers*, 173/318. Romanos (Paris) to Venizelos (London), October 17, 1922. Pioncaré's statement was probably a response to Romanos' request that provisions be made for the POW's and civil hostages in the Mudanya armistice convention.

the Greek males of military age, if Mustapha Kemal's attitude remained uncompromising, he should be told that "the Greek Government will proceed to take reprisals in the form of a male mobilization of the Musulmans in Greece." He apologized for the threat but felt that this was the only language the Turks understood.[38]

On October 19, Nansen left for Athens by car, inspecting refugee camps on the way. Three days later he reached the Greek capitol, where he met, as he did in Constantinople, with the ministers of the Allied powers and with the representatives of the foreign and Greek aid agencies. He also contacted the Greek government, which gave him full powers to negotiate with Turkey an immediate exchange of prisoners of war and of all the civilian hostages detained by the two governments and which expressed approval of the principle of a population exchange. It also gave Nansen a list of the Turkish prisoners of war and civilian hostages held by Greece. Understandably, it did not have a list of the Greek prisoners held by Turkey, but estimated that they numbered between 100,000 to 120,000 souls. Nansen also received assurances from the Greek government that if the civilian male hostages of military age were released by the Turks, they would not be enrolled in the Greek military and that Greece would cover the cost of the exchange.[39] Nansen also pressed Athens to draw up a scheme for the settlement of the refugees on the land and offered to send specialists in this field to Greece to help the government draw up the plan. He then returned to Constantinople to renew negotiations with the Angora government.[40]

---

[38]*Nansen Papers*, R 1761 (1922), 48/8441/24357, Venizelos (London) to Nansen (Constantinople), October 17, 1922.

[39]It is interesting to note that in 1920, a boat carrying 1,000 returning Turkish prisoners of war, after many years of captivity, from the Russian Far East was captured by a Greek warship. It was the time of the Greek-Turkish war and the Greeks interned them. Nansen, in his capacity of the League's High Commissioner for Prisoners of War, intervened and managed to have the Turkish POW's transferred to neutral territory. They were finally released and allowed to return to home on the express condition that Turkey agree not to use them in the war against Greece. Liv Nansen Høyer, *Nansen*, pp. 227–228.

[40]*Nansen Papers*, R 1761 (1922), 48/24929/24357. November 15, 1922, and R 1761 (1922), 48/24484/24375. R/78, November 1, 1922. For the report of Nansen's visit to Athens, see also *Venizelos Papers*, 29, Politis (Athens) to Venizelos (Paris), October 23, 1922.

*Fridtjof Nansen at the Acropolis, 1925*
*National Library of Norway, Picture Collection*

When he first arrived in Constantinople in early October, Nansen had several meetings with Hamid (Hâmit Hasancan), president of the Ottoman Red Crescent society and diplomatic representative in Constantinople of the Angora government, and had discussed with him the various problems concerning the question of the refugees. On October 14, Nansen sent a letter to Hamid outlining the various questions that he wished to take up with the Angora authorities and repeated his desire to enter into direct negotiations with his government. On the question of the male hostages detained by the Nationalists, Hamid volunteered that "because the Angora authorities regarded them as military hostages, he thought that they would be intransigent with regard to the proposal to release these men before the conclusion of a peace treaty."[41] Nansen's response, on the follow-

---

[41] *Nansen Papers*, R 1709 (1922), 42/24356/24034. October 15, 1922. "Note on a Conver-

ing day, was to send a direct appeal to the Turkish Grand National Assembly to release the hostages as soon as possible and not to wait for the conclusion of a peace treaty. He also sent a note to both governments to be magnanimous on this issue in the interest of the future peace in the Orient, and expressed the view that the advent of peace would be greatly assisted by the immediate exchange of prisoners of war and of all the civilian hostages detained by the two governments.[42] He received no reply.

The lack of progress on this front finally prompted Nansen to send, on November 2, a detailed memorandum on the refugee question to the Turkish government. While the memorandum was primarily concerned with movement on a population exchange agreement, it asked for a direct reply to the question whether or not Turkey was prepared to include the detained male refugees in such an agreement. He asked for a separate reply if the Angora government was willing to negotiate for an immediate exchange of prisoners of war and civil hostages as a matter apart from the exchange of populations.[43]

Over a week had passed with no response to his memorandum, and Nansen left for Geneva to submit his report and recommendations. By this time Nansen had come to the conclusion that immediate negotiations with Turkey on an exchange of populations seemed the only hopeful way of securing the freedom of the detained Greek hostages. All the issues that he tried so desperately to resolve on behalf of the refugees were left pending for the peace conference at Lausanne, where his efforts and recommendations on refugee issues were to serve as a useful guide for the deliberation of Allied powers and where Nansen laid down the ground work for an international refugee loan, indispensable for the settlement of the refugees in Greece. However, the suffering and anguish of the refugees, the prisoners of war, and the detained civilians continued unabated into the following year.

sation between Hamid Bey, President of the Ottoman Red Crescent, and Dr. Fridtjof Nansen, High Commissioner of the League for Refugees."

    [42]*Ibid.,* and *Nansen Papers,* R 1709 (1922), 48/24929/24357. November 15, 1922.

    [43]*Nansen Papers,* R 1761 (1922), 48/24318/24318. F. Nansen au Gouvernment de la Grande Assemblée Nationale de Turquie, November 3, 1922. Also in the same file letter of Nansen to Rumbold, the British High Commissioner in Constantinople, November 3, 1922.

# CHAPTER III

# The Nansen Negotiations for a Greek-Turkish Population Exchange

The mission of the relief agencies in the refugee crisis was to save lives, but not to extend relief indefinitely, nor to assume the primary burden of making the refugees self-sufficient. The latter was beyond their resources and mandate and raised a critical political question—where should the refugees be permanently settled so that they could regain their ability to be self-supporting? Consequently, by early November, in concert with Nansen, the relief agencies informed the League of Nations and the Allied High Commissioners in Constantinople that relief could not be extended indefinitely to the refugees and that they should start thinking of a permanent solution for the refugee problem. In the discussions that ensued, they expressed the belief that since Turkey would not allow the refugees, by now over one million souls, to return to their homes in safety, and since no one was prepared to force them to do so, the most likely solution to the problem would be the permanent settlement of the refugees on Greek soil and/or some kind of a Greek-Turkish population exchange.[1] Nansen's notion of the possibility of setting up autonomous regions for minorities within the Turkish state, areas to which the exiles could return with some semblance of security, or with international guarantees for the protection of minorities was completely unacceptable, not surprisingly, to the Turkish leadership.[2]

---

[1] *American Near East Relief Activities in Greece* (September 1922–December 1924), pp.1–3; and Clouzot, "La Société des Nations et les secours dans le Proche Orient," p. 961.

[2] Nansen tried on several occasions to get the Angora government to set up an autonomous district in eastern Anatolia for the few remaining survivors of the Armenian genocide, only to be adamantly rebuffed. Prior to the Mudanya armistice, there was even the suggestion for some kind of an autonomous state, under the League of Nations, in Eastern Thrace, for the protection of its Christian majority; and to serve as a buffer zone between Greece and Turkey. See *DBFP*, XVIII, Doc. 48. "British Secretary's Notes for a Conference between the French President of the Council, the British Secretary of State for Foreign

The defeat of the Greek army in Anatolia and the diplomatic isolation of Greece; the procrastination, rivalry, and indifference of the Allied powers; and the triumph of a Turkish nationalism bent on creating a homogeneous Turkish nation-state could not be ignored nor denied. These facts were obviously on the minds of those whose task it was to find a solution to the refugee problem, a solution that would produce peace in the region and a politically stable Greece. They were clearly expressed by Venizelos when he accepted the mandate of the Revolutionary Government to represent Greece abroad, but with the condition that it accept the loss of Eastern Thrace:

> The new government ought to know that the catastrophe we have been subjected to is irreparable. We have lost . . . Eastern Thrace, from the moment that the three Great Powers, once or formally our allies, have decided to yield themselves to Turkey. . . . We find ourselves in complete military and diplomatic isolation. . . . The Turks will do all they can to expel us from Western Thrace. . . . There remains one crucial question: to save the hundreds of thousands of Greeks, threatened with extermination by the return of the Turks to Europe. . . . This is why if the Government is invited to send a representative at Mudanya, it should at all costs refuse to evacuate Thrace before the signature of peace. . . . However, if its policy includes a resolution to hold on to Thrace, even against the decision taken by our former allies, I am afraid that I would have to decline the offer of representing my country abroad. . . .[3]

---

Affairs, and the Italian Ambassador in Paris, held at the Quai d'Orsay, September 20, 1922. There was also a last minute, desperate, but failed attempt by the Metropolitan of Smyrna, in the summer of 1922, to establish an autonomous Christian state in the Smyrna region under the sovereignty of the Ottoman Sultan, with perhaps Venizelos as High Commissioner.

[3] *Venizelos Papers*, 29, Venizelos (Paris) to the Greek Ministry of Foreign Affairs, October 1, 1922. The complete text is in Psomiades, "Eastern Thrace and the Armistice of Mudanya," pp. 25–26.

*Venizelos and the Revival of the Idea of a Population Exchange*

In the early hours of October 11, 1922, the Allied powers and Turkey reached an armistice agreement at Mudanya, after 10 grueling days of negotiations. But the Greek representative, General Mazarakis, refused to sign the agreement because of its omission of guarantees of amnesty, security, and minority rights for the Greek population remaining in Eastern Thrace, and in the absence of full instructions from his government. Accordingly, he left Mudanya for Athens. All eyes now turned to Venizelos.[4] On October 11, Simopoulos, the Greek High Commissioner in Constatinople, sent a frantic telegram to Venizelos asking that he be authorized to announce that the Greek government accepts the agreement and informing him of the warning of the British High Commissioner that Greece would be in great danger if it did not sign.[5] On the following day, Venizelos also received an urgent telegram from Athens asking him to immediately advise the government whether or not it should sign the armistice convention. Throughout the negotiations at Lausanne, Mazarakis received his instructions on the Greek position from Venizelos by way of Athens, which insisted that amnesty for the Greek population of Eastern Thrace should be included in the armistice agreement and that "if the Greek population wished to leave, it should have the right to do so, but only on a voluntary basis."[6]

---

[4]Eleftherios Venizelos (1864–1936) was Prime Minister of Greece during most of the period 1910–1920. He went into self-imposed exile in Paris after the disastrous electoral defeat of his party in November 1920. Military defeat in Asia Minor in September 1922 brought about the collapse of the royalist government, rebellion by elements of the Greek army and navy on September 24, 1922, and the installation of a Revolutionary Government in Athens by its leaders, primarily colonels Gonatas and Plastiras, on September 27–28, 1922. The goals of the Revolution were to hold on to Eastern Thrace, to remove and punish those responsible for the defeat in Asia Minor, and to deal with a rapidly deteriorating domestic situation that threatened the very integrity of the Greek state. Recognizing its own inexperience in foreign affairs, one of its first acts was to cable Venizelos, asking him to represent Greek interests abroad and providing him with full powers to deal with foreign policy questions. On the 29th the offer was accepted, just four days before the opening of the armistice negotiations at Mudanya. *Venizelos Papers*, 29, Revolutionary Committee (Athens) to Venizelos (Paris), September 27, 1922.

[5]*Venizelos Papers*, 29, Simopoulos (Constantinople) to Venizelos (London), October 11, 1922.

[6]*Venizelos Papers*, 29, Venizelos (Paris) to the Ministry of Foreign Affairs (Athens), October 8, 1922.

On October 12,Venizelos hurried to the British Foreign Office, seeking an official copy of the Mudanya convention, and met individually with Sir E. Crowe and Lord Curzon. Anticipating strong objections from Venizelos, the day before Crowe's meeting with Venizelos, Curzon met with Crowe and told him that "as the idea of expatriation is that of Venizelos and as he is here we should find out what he thinks or proposes before we thrust this task on the High Commissioners at Constantinople. . . . Please consult [with] him at once particularly on the W. Thrace proposal. The more Greeks can be got into W. Thrace and the more Turks and Bulgars extruded the easier will it be for Greece to retain her hold upon it."[7] Was Curzon suggesting a population exchange?[8]

[7] *DBFP*, XVIII, Doc. 122. Minute of Lord Curzon to Crowe on October 11, 1922 in *Record by Sir E. Crowe of a Conversation with M. Venizelos*, October 12, 1922. Curzon tried hard to insert into the Armistice text a meaningful provision, as promised to Venizelos, providing for the security of the Greek population of Eastern Thrace, but could not overcome the opposition of Turkey and of his French and Italian allies, whose support was viewed as indispensable to British interests. At this stage, the British position was to shift from a negative, failure to keep the promise to Venizelos, to a positive, the exit of the Greek population from Eastern Thrace will serve to strengthen Greece's position in Western Thrace.

[8] Perhaps Curzon was reminded of a Venizelos memo to the Peace Conference of 1919, in which Venizelos had suggested that in the event a portion of western Anatolia was given to Greece, it would be possible to arrange for a process of racial redistribution by a voluntary exchange of Greek and Turkish populations left stranded on the wrong side of the border, as has been done in the case of the Greeks and Bulgarians in eastern Roumeli, Macedonia, and Western Thrace. See A.A. Pallis, *Greece's Anatolian Venture and After: A Survey of the Diplomatic and Political Aspects of the Greek Expedition to Asia Minor (1915–1922)* (London: Methuen, 1937, pp. 58–59; and L.I. Paraskevopoulos, *Anamnisis* [Memoirs] (Athens, 1933), p. 362. The departure of the Greek population from Eastern Thrace was also anticipated by Curzon at a crucial meeting held by the Allied foreign ministers in Paris on October 6, 1922, following the temporary breakdown of the Mudanya negotiations. Curzon reminded his colleagues at the Paris meeting that Venizelos had agreed to the evacuation of the Greek army and administration from Eastern Thrace provided that the area remain under Allied administration until the signature of peace, for the protection of the Greek population, which, mindful of the Turkish atrocities in Asia Minor, would leave under difficult conditions. And in this case he asked who would feed and care for them? Otherwise, orderly arrangements must be made for the anticipated departure of the Greek population before the installation of the Turkish authorities. The French refused to be moved and displayed a cavalier attitude toward the plight of the refugees. Poincaré's response was that "the protection of minorities was of small relative importance . . . in any case, while the Turks might get excited in Asia, they would behave in Europe." *DBFP*, XVIII, Doc. 106. *British Secretary's Notes of a Meeting between the French President of Council, and the British Secretary of State for Foreign Affairs, and the Italian Chargé d" Affaires in Paris held in the Quai d'Orsay on October 6, 1922;* and Psomiades, "Eastern Thrace and the Armistice of Mudanya," p. 28.

Crowe took the matter up with Venizelos on October 12 and narrated the meeting on this issue as follows:

> I asked him whether he, or the Greek Government, had got any plans for carrying out this civilian evacuation [of Eastern Thrace]. He declared that there were no plans of any kind, and that, neither he nor anybody had any notion how, in practice, the withdrawal of a hundred thousand Greeks from [Eastern] Thrace into Greece proper was to be effected. No doubt it was imperative, but it was a problem which terrified him. He said that there were already half a million refugees arrived in Greece from Asia Minor; more were coming from the islands.... How many [of the remaining Greeks] might want to leave he could not say, but thought that there would be many. Where all these hundreds of thousands of people were to be put raised a physical problem of the greatest complexity. He had been thinking about it a good deal, and felt that he might be driven to some ruthless measures, such as ordering all Greek villages and towns to set aside one-half, or a certain proportion, of their buildings for the incoming families, forcing the inhabitants to huddle together as best they could in the remaining accommodations. I asked him whether he had considered the possibility of now proceeding with a plan, of which I knew he had been in favour formerly, as regards Bulgaria and Macedonia, namely, the interchange of Greek and Moslem populations. He would no doubt himself have realized that there might be a technical advantage for Greece to have in Western Thrace as many Greeks coming from Eastern Thrace as possible. If the Turks of Western Thrace, and perhaps of Thessaly, were ready to migrate to Eastern Thrace in return, this would offer some means of finding room for the refugees. M. Venizelos said that he did not overlook this possibility, but apart from the question of making arrangements for such an elaborate exchange within the short time available ... such a scheme would only offer a very partial alleviation of the difficulty.[9]

[9] *DBFP*, XVIII, Doc. 122. *Record of Sir E. Crowe of a Conversation with M. Venizelos,* October 12, 1922.

On the following day, having received the Mudanya text, Venizelos met with Curzon and bitterly complained of the shabby treatment of Greece by its former allies and their complete indifference to the fate of the Greek population of Eastern Thrace. Nevertheless, following the exhortations of Curzon (who sought to assure him that one way or another the Greek population of Eastern Thrace would be protected) and with the need for Allied support at the forthcoming peace conference in mind, Venizelos advised a reluctant Greek leadership that it was in the interest of Greece to accept the verdict of Mudanya. On October 13, 1922, Athens officially accepted the terms of the armistice and instructed High Commissioner Simopoulos to address a declaration to the Allied High Commissioners in Constantinople and to the Government of the Grand National Assembly of Turkey signifying Greece's acceptance of the Mudanya convention. The text of the declaration, prepared by Venizelos, read as follows:

> The Greek Government considers that its declarations made by the Greek delegates at Mudanya should have been taken into consideration, especially regarding guarantees and formulas necessary for the safety of the lives and property of the Christian population of Eastern Thrace. The Greek Government makes a final appeal to the sentiments of humanity of the Allied Powers in favor of these populations. Desiring, nevertheless, to conform to the decision of the Powers, the Greek Government sees itself obliged to submit and declare its adherence to the armistice protocol signed at Mudanya.[10]

At the same time, prompted by that verdict and by the anticipated exodus of the Greek population of Eastern Thrace, Venizelos requested from Athens the number of Turks living in Greece and sent a telegram to Nansen in which he decisively accepted the permanent

---

[10] *DBFP*, XVIII, Doc.124, Lindley (Athens) to Curzon (London), October 13, 1922; Alexander Mazarakis-Ainian, *Memoires* (Thessaloniki, 1979), p. 299; France, Ministères des Relations Extèrieures, Series "E", 1919–1929, *Levant: Turquie*, Tel. 1499 [E340–1]. Pellé (Constantinople) to Poincaré (Paris), October 12, 1922; and *Venizelos Papers*, 29, Kanellopoulos (Athens) to Venizelos (London), October 14, 1922.

settlement of the refugees in Greece.[11] And to achieve this radical solution to the refugee problem, Venizelos combined an appeal for foreign assistance and a population exchange:

> I am glad to learn you have accepted the mission entrusted you by the League of Nations to go to the Near East as its Commissioner and to undertake the work of succoring hundreds of thousands of refugees. This noble and important mission could not have been placed in more capable hands. Total number of refugees, who recent events are forcing them to leave their homes and who will take refuge on Greek soil and ask shelter and means of livelihood, will exceed million by far. The Greek state which is just emerging from ten years period of war and is exhausted is not in position to meet these colossal demands. The sympathy enterprise and material assistance of the world is necessary in order that this relief work be brought to successful issue. Minister of Interior of Angora Government declared fortnight ago [September 29, 1922] that Turks are decided not to allow further presence of Greeks on Turkish soil and will propose at forthcoming conference the compulsory exchange of Greek and Turkish populations. As the question of housing of refugees will be even more difficult than that of their alimentation particularly with the approach of winter, I take the liberty of requesting that you will endeavor to arrange that transfer of populations begin before the signature of peace. Taking into account that in Greece today there are about 350,000 Turks and that these could be immediately transferred to houses and properties of the Christians of Asia Minor who have already left and those of Thrace, who are about to leave, it would be possible to provide housing for proportionate number of Greek refugees and the problem of their accommodation would be so facilitated.[12]

---

[11] *AYE*, 1922: 88(6)1,1, Caclamanos (London) to the Greek Ministry of Foreign Affairs, October 13, 1922. The figure he was given was 450,000. This request could suggest that Venizelos had in mind some kind of a population exchange.

[12] *Nansen Papers*, R 1761 (1922), 48/24318/24318, Venizelos (London) to Nansen (Constantinople), October 13, 1922; also in *Venizelos Papers,* 29, Caclamanos (London) to Simopoulos (Constantinople), October 13, 1922.

The interpretation of this telegram has been the subject of much debate by scholars. Ladas, commenting on the cable, deduced that "Venizelos was proposing a total exchange, and probably a compulsory one, since he was calculating on the immediate transfer of all Turks from Greece," as a partial solution for the refugee housing problem.[13] Pentzopoulos, on the other hand, while agreeing with Ladas to the extent that Venizelos was thinking in terms of an accord covering minorities of the entire two countries and not select geographical provinces, believed that "it could not be substantiated that Venizelos envisaged an obligatory exchange and indeed that subsequent events proved that he was against the forceful transfer of populations."[14] Svolopoulos argued that the cable of October 13 "did not give a clear response to the question who initiated the idea of a compulsory population exchange," but that "its deepest meaning implied a compulsory exchange."[15] Koufa and Svolopoulos agreed that Venizelos, without actually stating it in so many words, had essentially adopted the term "compulsory exchange," and that Nansen, taking his cue from the Venizelos telegram, "undertook to promote the solution that had been proposed by Venizelos, but actually imposed by the Turkish government's action of expelling the Greeks from Turkish territory."[16] Nansen's belief, conveyed to Venizelos, that if the exchange was not compulsory, the Muslims would not leave Greece voluntarily, undoubtedly influenced his critique of Venizelos' telegram.[17] In any case, the statement that the bulk of the Muslims would not leave Greece voluntarily was not exactly a revelation to Venizelos. Why should they leave? They had not been subject to

---

[13]Ladas, *The Exchange of Minorities*, p. 336.

[14]Pentzopoulos, *The Balkan Exchange of Minorities and its Impact upon Greece*, p. 63.

[15]Svolopoulos, *I apofasi gia tin ypohreotiki andalagi ton plithismon metaxi Ellados kai Tourkias*, p. 7, 20.

[16]Kalliopi K. Koufa and Constantine Svolopoulos, "The Compulsory Exchange of Populations between Greece and Turkey: The Settlement of the Minority Questions at the Conference of Lausanne, 1923, and its Impact on Greek-Turkish Relations," in *Ethnic Groups in International Relations*, Vol. 5, edited by Paul Smith in collaboration with Kalliopi Koufa and Arnold Suppan (New York: New York University Press, 1991), p. 297.

[17]*AYE*, 1922: 88(2)1,1, Simopoulos (Constantinople) to Politis (Athens), October 20, 1922.

atrocities and persecutions. Throughout the entire war, the policy of the Greek government, initiated by Venizelos himself, was that minorities should be respected and enjoy all of the rights of Greek citizenship. They were to live peacefully in their homes and not to be interfered with in any way. This policy, which was strictly implemented, was in part motivated by Venizelos' desire to demonstrate to the Great Powers that Greece could rule impartially over areas of mixed populations, and undoubtedly, by the imperative of almost a century of Greek liberal ideology and democratic politics.[18]

The fact of the matter is that the term "compulsory exchange" had not yet entered the vocabulary of international discourse. Voluntary exchanges of populations, nevertheless, are seldom really voluntary. In crisis situations, or as in the Greek case, where there occurred a massive expulsion of a population prior to an agreement on population exchange and the state was unable to provide for them, the element of coercion comes into play. When an incoming population, having been rudely and forcefully uprooted and stripped of its possessions, finds itself without shelter and the means of livelihood in the receiving country, it is likely to move on a settled minority population that is identified with its former tormentors. In such cases, the element of coercion is difficult, if not impossible, to contain, even if it is not state sanctioned. Such an eventuality, with all of its ramifications (international condemnation and the threat of the resumption of hostilities by Turkey) could not have escaped the thoughts of Venizelos in his telegram to Nansen on October 13.

The meaning of that telegram to Nansen can also be grasped by Venizelos' response to a note two days later from Efthemios Kanellopoulos, the Greek foreign minister, asking him should the govern-

---

[18]During this period, the Muslims were not drafted into military service. They freely elected their local officials, including the Muslim mayor of Thessaloniki. In the national elections of November 1920, they sent more than 20 Turkish deputies to the Greek parliament, and because of the great division in Greek politics, their influence was greatly felt. There were also many Muslim mayors even in cities and villages with a predominant Greek population. Up to 1922, the mayor of Thessaloniki was a Muslim. Seferiades, *L'échange des populations*, p. 49. See also George T. Mavrokordatos, *Stillborn Republic: Social Coalitions and Party Strategies in Greece, 1922–1936* (Berkeley: University of California Press, 1982).

ment discourage the Greeks of Eastern Thrace from abandoning their homes and fleeing to Greece?[19] His reply was unequivocal:

> I think that the Government would be committing a grave crime if it did not help the population of Eastern Thrace that wished to emigrate. Of course, if it were possible to secure their life and property until the conclusion of peace, we would be in a better position at the peace conference to negotiate a population exchange. But it is absolutely certain that after 30 days, with the removal of all Allied controls on the Turkish administration in Thrace, the Turks will plunder the movable property of our fellow countrymen and will expel them naked and miserable. Remember what happened on the eve of the Great War. Today, this will be repeated on a much larger scale because of the contempt the Turks have of the Great Powers. For this reason, it is necessary to facilitate in every way the departure of our fellow countrymen, taking with them their movable property before the [Turkish] army comes.... Do not deceive yourself! Eastern Thrace is lost forever for Hellenism. The Turks will not tolerate a compact alien population, especially at the very gates of their capital. The problem of settling so many thousands of refugees is of course terrifying but we cannot avoid it. . . . There is hope that all the world will help. Upon a proper solution of this problem depends the future of Greece and the security of our borders beyond the Aliakmonos. It is clear that with the withdrawal of the Greek population of Eastern Thrace we will be forced to ask the Turks in Greece to leave Greece to make room for the incoming refugees. But it should be done in a civilized way by the League of Nations and managed by Dr. Nansen.[20]

Venizelos then asked that the decision for the departure of the Turkish population from Greece remain a secret until the complete evacuation of Eastern Thrace and further advised that the government should make an appeal on his behalf to the Greek population not to destroy their abandoned homes upon their departure from

---

[19] *Venizelos Papers*, 30, Kanellopoulos (Athens) to Venizelos (London), October 15, 1922.
[20] *Venizelos Papers*, 30, Venizelos (London) to Kanellopoulos (Athens), October 16, 1922.

Eastern Thrace. Such an act, he told Kanellopoulos, would make their settlement in Greece easier because it would ultimately facilitate the orderly evacuation of the Turkish population from their homes in Greece by providing them with the abandoned Greek homes in Eastern Thrace.

On the following day, October 17, heeding the advice of Venizelos, a directive was dispatched to the Governor General of Eastern Thrace that the army and civil population should refrain from destroying the abandoned houses.[21] The directive was also a response to Nansen's request that the Greek government use all in its power to prevent the destruction of property and homes in Eastern Thrace, in spite of the provocations by Muslim civilians and armed bands. Such destruction, he warned, would severely compromise his efforts on behalf of the refugees.[22]

Venizelos' great concern was to clear Greece of its Muslim population to make room for the mass of Greek refugees. He realized instinctively that Greece could not do it without Turkey's permission, and that there would be severe repercussions if Greece forced the expulsion of its Turkish minority. It would undermine his ability to negotiate an international refugee loan. It would further isolate Greece at the scheduled peace conference, upon whose outcome the future of Greece would depend. It would probably lead to the renewal of Greek-Turkish hostilities. And it certainly would accelerate the massacres and expulsions of the remaining 200,000 Greeks in Anatolia and even those in Constantinople. What would happen to the Greek detainees, prisoners of war, and civilian hostages held by the Turks?

Meanwhile, the Turkish ports were filled with sick and hungry Greek refugees, seeking a safe haven; the victims of the ongoing policy of the Kemalists to unilaterally evict them from their homes and drive them out of the country. With the new huge inflow of refugees

---

[21] *AYE*, 1922:88(2)1,1. Greek Ministry of Foreign Affairs to the Governor General (Adrianople). October 17, 1922.

[22] *AYE*, 1922: 88(2)1,1. Simopoulos (Constantinople) to Ministry of Foreign Affairs (Athens). Telegram of Nansen to Venizelos, October 17, 1922.

from Eastern Thrace, the Pontos, and the interior of Anatolia, Venize-los became increasingly apprehensive that the Turks would delay, if not refuse, an agreement for a population exchange. He was also greatly disturbed by developments in Greece, where the Revolution-ary Government appeared overwhelmed by the problem of caring for the refugees and by the need to sustain its military forces for the defense of Western Thrace. There were also alarming indications that the government was pulling back from its agreements with Venizelos accepting the loss of Eastern Thrace and the need for a population exchange.[23] Particularly disturbing to Venizelos was the idea, widely circulating in Athens, that it would be better if the refugees returned to Turkey at whatever the cost.[24] And in fact many refugees continued to harbor the notion of returning to their former homes.[25]

Thus, Venizelos was confronted by problems with both Angora and Athens, which could only be resolved, in his view, by obtaining an immediate agreement for a Greek-Turkish population exchange. He was fearful that if Greece did not reach an agreement with Angora soon, before the Christian element was completely expelled from Turkey, Athens' ability to effect a satisfactory exchange would be sig-nificantly limited. Moreover, he dared not contemplate the alterna-tive of forcefully removing the Muslim population from Greek territory without the consent of Turkey, which, in his view, would be morally reprehensible and, as earlier noted, politically disastrous for Greece.[26] There was also the fear that such an action would provoke irresistible pressures on Angora to occupy Constantinople (which was to remain under Allied occupation until a peace treaty was signed) and slaughter and/or expel its sizeable Greek population.[27]

[23] *Venizelos Papers,* 29, Venizelos (London) to Plastiras (Athens), October 14, 1922.

[24] *Nansen Papers,* R 1761 (1922), 48/24318/24318. Letter of Baker (Athens) to Nansen (Constantinople), October 14, 1922; Milton Pagtziloglou, *I genoktonia ton Ellinon kai ton Armenion tis Mikras Asias* [The genocide of the Greeks and Armenians in Asia Minor] (Athens, 1988), pp. 218–219. The substance of these indications were also reflected in the Kanellopoulos–Venizelos exchanges of October 15 and 16, referred to earlier in the text.

[25] *AYE, 1922:* 88(2)1,2. Rentis (Athens) to Venizelos (Lausanne), December 10, 1922.

[26] *Venizelos Papers,* 30, Venizelos (London) to the Greek Ministry of Foreign Affairs, October 17, 1922.

[27] *Venizelos Papers,* 30, Venizelos (London) to the Greek Ministry of Foreign Affairs, October 17, 1922.

In fact, Hamid, the representative of the Angora government in Constantinople, told Nansen that if the Greeks expel the Turks from Greece, "we will massacre all of the remaining Greeks, including those in Constantinople."[28] Even without state sanction for such a policy, one way or another the Muslims of Greece would probably bear more than their fair share of the burden of resettling the refugees, inviting a strong reaction from Angora as well as from the international community.

For Venizelos, the very integrity of the Greek state depended upon a calm calculation of the new reality and the need to absorb over one million refugees. He made every effort and used every possible argument to convince his countrymen of this urgent imperative. In his memorandum to the Greek government on October 17, he stressed that "the future of Greece, without exaggeration, depends on the good or bad solution of this question [of the refugees]. Failure of reaching the good solution will cause disasters one is terrified to contemplate, while success will contribute in a few years to our rise from the unbearable burdens which we inherited from the unfortunate ending of the war and to securing, after the demise of the Greater Greece, a Great Greece, whose borders will never be secure if Western Thrace and Macedonia will not become ethnically, as well as politically, Greek."[29] The memorandum was typical of the strategic arguments Venizelos employed to convince the Greek leadership, particularly the nationalists and the military, that the security of the geographically sensitive regions of northern Greece could only be realized by a mutually acceptable population exchange with Turkey. But his primary motive for seeking a population exchange was much more than simply a ploy to reinforce the Greek population of northern Greece. It was, as he clearly stated in the above memorandum, to help bring stability to a financially exhausted, politically fractured and socially agitated Greece by quickly facilitating the awesome and necessary task of settling the refugees, who were well over twenty per-

---

[28] *Venizelos Papers*, 31, Politis (Athens) to Venizelos (London), November 9, 1922.
[29] *Venizelos Papers*, 30, Venizelos (London) to the Greek Ministry of Foreign Affairs, October 17, 1922.

cent of the country's population, and to ameliorate the country's anomalous and dangerous relations with Turkey.

On October 17, in response to his anxieties over developments in both Greece and Turkey and the festering problem of the refugees, Venizelos cabled Nansen that it was imperative that Turkey "should, as quickly as possible, be persuaded to give its consent to the speedy transfer of the Turks now in Greece.... Perhaps, if reasons of a higher order fail to persuade Mustapha Kemal, it will be possible for you to point out to him that if he does not concur in the migration of the Turks from Greece, the Greek Government under pressure of unavoidable necessity will be very probably compelled to impose this migration on the Turks living on Greek soil. . . ."[30]

## The Nansen Initiative

Venizelos' telegram of October 13 was dispatched before the arrival of Nansen's telegram of October 10, which independently recommended the settlement of the Greek refugees on vacant lands in Macedonia and Western Thrace and vaguely suggested a Greek-Turkish population exchange:

> ... Everyone appears to agree that it is hopeless to expect that Turkey will agree to receive them again in Asia Minor, or that the refugees themselves would agree to go even if they were received back in. They must be therefore settled elsewhere and I presume that it will be the purpose of the Greek Government either as a result of treaty for the exchange of populations with the Turkish Government, or without such a treaty to settle them in the vacant lands of Macedonia and Western Thrace—the vast numbers of refugees will have to be settled on land that is neither occupied or cultivated. The alternative to settling the refugees is to support them in idleness for perhaps 2–3 years, which must be unacceptable to the Greek Government and the voluntary agencies. What is needed is rapid settlement on vacant land in the interest of world peace. . . .[31]

[30]*Nansen Papers*, R 1761 (1922), 48/84441/24357. October 17. 1922.
[31]*AYE*, 1922: 88(2)1,1. Nansen(Constantinople) to Venizelos (Paris), October 10, 1922;

Nansen also informed Venizelos that it was possible for the League of Nations to assist his government in a policy of settling the refugees on vacant lands in northern Greece. The League could assist Greece by securing for it the support of various charities and/or by helping it obtain a foreign loan for carrying through a settlement policy—and even by providing assistance for the administration of such a loan. To get the loan, Nansen advised that the Greek government should make the world understand that it recognizes that the rapid and successful solution of the refugee problem was absolutely essential for the future of Greece.

We do not have here an endorsement by Nansen of a population exchange agreement; that was to come later, after receiving Venizelos' telegram of October 13. At this stage, Nansen is not prepared to consider the settlement of the refugees by uprooting Greece's Muslim population. However, Nansen, not surprisingly, argued that if getting rid of its Muslim population were on the mind of the Greek government, it should be the result of a treaty with Turkey. Nansen was in Constantinople less than a week, when after careful consideration, he came to the conclusion that the refugees would not be allowed to return to their homes in peace, and therefore, in the interest of their well-being, they should be settled in Greece. They should be taken off the dole and made self-sufficient.

Upon obtaining Veniselos' telegram of October 13, Nansen immediately wired the Secretary General of the League that he had "received official request from Venizelos to organize an immediate exchange of Greek and Turkish populations of Thrace, Macedonia and Asia Minor without awaiting signature of peace. As this is essentially a question within the scope of refugee work and vital to satisfactory solution of existing problems consider impossible to refuse to act on this definite request of Member of League although this involves increased responsibility ... impossible to wait Council's consideration as immediate action is essential. . . . "[32] Nansen was obvi-

and *Nansen Papers,* R1761 (1922), 48/84441/24357, Nansen (Constantinople) to Venizelos (Paris), October 10, 1922.
   [32]Great Britain, Public Record Office (PRO), FO 371/7956, E 11589, London, October

ously pressing for an elastic interpretation of the scope of the mission with which he was charged by the League. On October 16, Nansen again informed the League of Venizelos' request that he:

> . . . endeavour to arrange an immediate exchange of the Greek and Turkish populations of Macedonia, Thrace and Asia Minor. In making this request M. Venizelos refers to a declaration made a short time ago by the Minister of Interior of the Nationalist Government of Angora, to the effect that the Government had decided not to allow the further presence of Greeks on Turkish soil, and that it would accordingly propose at the forthcoming conference of peace the *compulsory* exchange of the Greek and Turkishpopulations. M. Venizelos requests me to endeavour to arrange *such* an exchange shall begin as soon as possible and that negotiations *to this end* shall be carried on independently of the negotiations for peace. (Italics added)[33]

Venizelos' cable of October 13 appears to be interpreted by Nansen as a clear indication that the Greek statesman had accepted the principle of a compulsory population exchange.

Meanwhile, with the conclusion of the Mudanya armistice, the Allied High Commissioners in Constantinople had decided that the League of Nations was the suitable body to undertake the orderly evacuation of the Greek population that wished to leave Eastern Thrace and the exchange of prisoners of war between Greece and Turkey.[34] On October 15, Nansen, as the League's High Commissioner for refugees and POWs, was asked to take on these tasks. On the same day, Nansen presented to the High Commissioners (Britain, France, Italy and Japan) in Constantinople the Venizelos letter of October 13, which they immediately endorsed without qualifica-

14, 1922. The cable was sent by Rumbold, the British High Commissioner in Constantinople, for Drummond (Geneva) from Nansen (Constantinople). See also F. Nansen, "Refugees and the Exchange of Populations," *The Encyclopedia Britannica*, 14th printing, Vol. 19 (London, 1929), pp. 58–60.

[33] *Nansen Papers*, R 1761 (1922), 48/24318/24318. "Exchanges of Greek and Turkish Populations and of Prisoners and Civilian Hostages," Nansen (Constantinople) to Drummond (Geneva), October 16, 1922.

[34] *DBFP*, XVIII, Doc. 26. Rumbold (Constantinople) to Curzon (London), October 16, 1922.

tions. They too were anxious to settle quickly the exchange of populations and not wait for the conclusion of the anticipated long diplomatic negotiations at Lausanne. Therefore, after brief discussions, the Allied High Commissioners formally invited Nansen "to take all possible steps to endeavor to reach an agreement with regard to an exchange of population between the Greek and Turkish governments as soon as possible, independently of the peace negotiations." They had conveniently concluded, with some prodding from Nansen, that the question of the refugees was essentially connected with that of an eventual exchange of minorities.[35] "So it was technically true to say that Nansen was merely acting on behalf of the Allies when he promoted the two-way population transfer; but it was a mandate that he actively sought."[36]

### The Nansen Negotiations with Turkey for a Population Exchange

From the very beginning of his stay in Constantinople, Nansen had made every effort to secure immediate contact with the Angora authorities, only to be rebuffed or ignored. He had earlier met with Hamid, the Nationalist representative in Constantinople, explaining his mission and his urgent need for an appointment with Kemal, but with no results. However, on October 15, with his new mandate from the Allied powers and Greece to secure an agreement on a population exchange, he again pressed Hamid for a meeting with Kemal.[37]

The meeting with Hamid apparently reinforced Nansen's optimism in securing an agreement for a population exchange. It led him to inform Venizelos that, although he did not mention to Hamid

[35]*AYE*, 1922: 88(2)1,1. Simopoulos (Constantinople) to the Greek Ministry of Foreign Affairs (for Venizelos from Nansen), October 15, 1922; and *Nansen Papers,* R 1761, 48/24929/24357, "L'oeuvre de Docteur Nansen," October 15, 1922. The High Commissioners assured Nansen of their support and that of their governments in the Council of the League of Nations for a population exchange.

[36]Bruce Clark, *Twice a Stranger: The Mass Expulsions that Forged Modern Greece and Turkey* (London: Granta Books, 2006), p. 52.

[37]*Nansen Papers,* R 1761 (1922), 48/24318/24318. Nansen (Constantinople) to Drummond (Geneva), October 16, 1922. See also *Ibid.*, Nansen (Constantinople to Venizelos (London), October 15, 1922 and *Venizelos Papers,* 29, Nansen (Constantinople) to Venizelos (London), October 16, 1922.

*Miniature of Fridtjof Nansen*
*National Library of Norway, Picture Collection*

Greece's official request for a population exchange, believing that it was preferable for him to come into direct negotiations with Kemal, Hamid had freely voiced the opinion that his government was extremely favorable to such a proposal and that Nansen left the meeting "almost certain that it [the Angora government] will agree to face the question immediately."[38]

While waiting for an appointment with Kemal, Nansen went to Sophia and Athens on urgent business in connection with refugee relief. In his brief visit to Athens on October 22, Nansen also obtained confirmation of the Greek government's decision that he should attempt to secure an agreement on the exchange of populations. He advised Athens to draw up a scheme for the settlement of the rural refugees on the vacant lands in Macedonia and Thrace. This advice, according to Nansen, was well received because the government was anxious to keep the destitute refugees out of the cities, if at all possible, to avoid social unrest.[39]

Upon his return to Constantinople on October 23, Nansen received a telegram, dated October 22, from Kemal stating that "the exchange proposed by Dr. Nansen is acceptable in principle, however, it is necessary to take up the matter with the Government. As it is impossible for me under present conditions to wait in any one town, it is unfortunately not possible for me to fix a meeting place."[40] Despite his great disappointment at the indefinite postponement of consultations with Angora, the ever persistent Nansen, mindful of the humanitarian nightmare looming over Greece, again renewed his efforts to meet with the Turkish leadership. On October 24, Nansen called upon Refet [Bele], the newly appointed Nationalist Governor of Thrace, who had just arrived at Constantinople, for assistance in securing an appointment with Angora. In the interview, Refet suggested that in order to reach a speedy agreement on the population exchange, Nansen should proceed without further delay to Angora and promised that Hamid would inform Nansen as soon as the necessary arrangements for the journey have been made. Refet also informed Nansen that he would need a document stating that the Greek government had given him full powers to negotiate a population exchange agreement. Nansen consequently procured this document by telegraph.[41]

Nansen's fears that his departure for Angora would be postponed was only too well founded. Four days later, dissatisfied with the slow-

[39] *Venizelos Papers*, 29, Politis (Athens) to Venizelos (Paris), October 23, 1922. The cable was a report of Nansen's meeting with the Greek government. Nansen's activities in Greece and Turkey were widely covered by the Turkish press, which reported on October 22 that Greece had agreed to a population exchange. Onur Yildirim, *Diplomats and Refugees: Mapping the Turco-Greek Exchange of Populations, 1922–1924* (Ph.D. Dissertation, Princeton University, 2002), pp. 76–77.

[40] *Nansen Papers*, R 1761 (1922), 48/24318/24318. Report of Dr. Nansen, Part I, *Reciprocal Exchange of Racial Minorities between Greece and Turkey* (Geneva), November 15, 1922.

[41] *Ibid.*

ness of the process, he arranged for another interview with Refet, who promised that he would take personal steps in the matter and assured Nansen that a reply concerning his trip would be forthcoming in two days. According to Nansen's aide, Noel-Baker, some of the arguments of Venizelos were used in the encounter with Refet. Nansen told Refet that "the Greek government from sheer lack of living space might feel obliged to expel the half a million Turks; if a treaty was made which he [Nansen] prepared, those Turks would be moved under the supervision of an international commission, the value of their lands would be impartially assessed and when they arrived in Turkey they would receive full payment for everything they left behind. In any case Turkey would add new citizens to fill the towns and villages which the Greeks had fled."[42]

Nansen waited until October 30 for a reply to the proposal that he had made to proceed to Angora. On that date, he sent his aides de Roover and Burnier to meet with Refet, who informed them that he had received the long awaited reply. It was from Hussein Raouf [Orbay], President of the Turkish Council of Ministers, stating that the Turkish government was "in principle favorable to an exchange of populations, excluding [the Muslims] of Western Thrace," and that the government, desirous of saving Nansen from a journey to Angora, had charged its representative in Constantinople to negotiate the details with him.[43] A copy of the telegram was given to Nansen by Hamid, along with a copy of a telegram from Ismet [Inönü], the newly appointed Turkish Minister of Foreign Affairs, informing Hamid that "there is no need for Dr. Nansen to go to Angora. We agree to the exchange of populations. On this principle you can discuss with Dr. Nansen."[44]

---

[42]Quoted from Clark, *Twice a Stranger,* p. 58; and Yildirim, *Diplomats and Refugees,* p. 78.

[43]*Nansen Papers,* R 1761 (1922), 48/24318/24318, Colban (Constantinople) to Drummond (Geneva), October 31, 1922.

[44]*Ibid.* Report by Dr Nansen, Part I, *Reciprocal Exchange of Racial Minorities between Greece and Turkey* (Geneva), November 15, 1922. The document was also circulated by the Secretary General of the League, Sir Eric Drummond, to the League Council, Member States and the Secretariat: The League of Nations, *The Question of Exchange of Populations between Greece and Turkey* (Geneva), November 15, 1922, C.736/M447.

The telegram of Hussein Rauf seems to imply a compulsory population exchange by excepting Western Thrace. This is also the first time that an exception to a population exchange is explicitly mentioned. Western Thrace was left out because the official position of the Turkish government, in accordance with paragraph three of its National Pact, was that "the determination of the juridical status of Western Thrace, which had been made dependent on the Turkish peace, must be effected in accordance with the votes which shall be given the inhabitants in complete freedom."[45] In other words, there will be a Turkish demand at the Lausanne peace conference that the future of Western Thrace be decided by plebiscite. If the plebiscite were to be denied, the substantial Muslim population would remain in Western Thrace, within reach of the Turkish fatherland, and could one day be united with Turkey, given the right circumstances.[46]

Nansen was clearly unhappy with the responses from Angora and expressed his fears to his colleagues that the instructions given to Hamid would not enable him to enter into really fruitful negotiations. Yet, he could not refuse the invitation to deal with Hamid. On October 31, the meeting took place with Nansen, assisted by his staff of experts—de Roover, Burnier, Baker and Colban—and Hamid, who was not accompanied by any secretary or supporting staff, in Nansen's hotel, the Pera Palace. It was to be Nansen's first and last official conference with Hamid. The Turkish representative wasted no time in bringing the negotiations to a standstill. He started the discussions by observing that Nansen's *pleins pouvoirs* did not men-

---

[45]Tevfik Bıyıklıoğlu, *Trakya'da milli mücadele* [The national struggle in Thrace], Vol. 2 (Ankara: Türk Tarih Kurumu Basimevi, 1956), pp. 124–125, 194–195. For the text of the National Pact of January 28, 1920 see Eliot G. Mears, *Modern Turkey: A Politico-Economic Interpretation, 1908–1923* (New York: Macmillan, 1924), pp. 629–631.

[46]Kemal Atatürk, *A Speech Delivered by Ghazi Mustapha Kemal, October 1927* (Leipzig: K. F. Koehler, 1929), p. 351, hereafter cited as *The Speech*. Turkey lost most of Western Thrace during the Balkan Wars of 1912–1913 to Bulgaria. On September 6, 1915, the Ottoman government gave Bulgaria the remaining portion of Western Thrace for entering the World War on the side of the Central Powers, of which Turkey was a member. Greece acquired Western Thrace from Bulgaria by the treaty of Neuilly (1919). However, the Turkish Nationalists considered Eastern and Western Thrace as one unit belonging to Turkey. For the struggle for Thrace, see Psomiades, *The Eastern Question*, pp. 39–50; Psomiades, "Eastern Thrace and the Armistice of Mudanya," pp. 1–67; and Smith, *Ionian Vision*.

tion Constantinople, which should come under the exchange scheme. He then informed Nansen that his instructions only permitted him to negotiate on the basis of a total and compulsory exchange of populations, excepting the Muslims of Western Thrace, but from which the population of Constantinople would not be excluded. This is the first time that the term *compulsory* appeared in the official negotiations for a population exchange.

Nansen objected to the limitation of the discussion set by Hamid, although he thought that a compulsory exchange as a solution was not altogether excluded.[47] And Hamid responded that in his opinion, it was useless to continue the discussions without further instructions from his government. It was agreed, however, that Hamid would wire Angora and ask for instructions as to whether he could proceed with the discussions on the basis of voluntary emigration. And at the same time, Nansen would wire Athens and ask whether it would authorize him to negotiate on the basis of compulsory emigration, including Constantinople. Up to this point the question whether the exchange was to be obligatory or voluntary had not been discussed by any of the parties, although the implications of a forced exchange had been present. Nansen was only thinking of a voluntary exchange, similar to that of the 1919 treaty between Greece and Bulgaria, which reinforced the Greek population of Western Thrace.

Fearful of further delays in resolving the refugee crisis, Nansen suggested that the discussions continue while waiting for a reply by the two governments, as many of the details in a population exchange would be more or less the same if one or the other alternative was finally adopted. He gave Hamid a list of questions that would have to be discussed. However, as was to be expected, Hamid demurred and showed the greatest reluctance to enter into further deliberations. His rebuttal to Nansen was that it would be a waste of time and labor to continue the talks before knowing the position of the two governments on the fundamental question of compulsory or voluntary

---

[47] *Nansen Papers*, R 1761 (1922), 48/24929/24357. "The Work of Doctor Nansen Concerning the Organization of Aid to Refugees in the Near East," November 15, 1922.

emigration. Moreover, he complained that he had no experts at his disposal, they were busy elsewhere, while Nansen's staff was free to give full attention to the issue. Therefore, he would be personally in a position of inferiority in any discussion relating to technical details. The end result was, at the insistence of Nansen, an agreement that he would send to Hamid a document on the following day containing a preliminary draft agreement on a population exchange, which might serve as a more detailed basis for discussion than the list of questions. But Nansen failed to draw from Hamid a clearer idea of when an agreement could possibly be ready for signature.[48]

On November 1, 1922, as scheduled, de Roover and Colban called upon Hamid to hand him the draft stipulations for an exchange agreement and tried to arrange a meeting to review and explain the document, only to be told by Hamid that he himself could no longer deal with the issue because he had to leave in three days for the peace conference at Lausanne. He added that he had asked Angora to appoint a substitute and to send experts to Constantinople for the resumption of the discussions and hoped to have a reply to his request within three or four days.[49] Nansen's assistants were also informed that the basis of an eventual accord could only be an integral and obligatory exchange of populations and that Angora "did not consider the issue to have a character of urgency and that its examination could wait until after the conclusion of the Peace Conference."[50] Understandably, the greater priority of Kemal and his lieutenants was to deal immediately with the aftermath of the Greek defeat and to strengthen their hold on their country in the face of the unraveling of the war time coalition or Nationalist movement. It was time now to consolidate their power.

---

[48]*Nansen Papers*, R 1761 (1922), 48/24318/24318, Colban (Constantinople) to Drummond (Geneva), October 31, 1922. Nansen's aides, de Roover and Colban, were asked by their chief to draw up the preliminary draft agreement, given their extensive experience with a similar agreement between Greece and Bulgaria.

[49]*Ibid.*

[50]*Nansen Papers*, R 1761 (1922), 48/24929/24357, "L'oeuvre du Docteur Nansen," November 15, 1922.

*The Greek Response*

Meanwhile, Nansen sent an urgent cable to Politis, the Greek Minister for Foreign Affairs, apprizing him of the results of the October 31 meeting with Hamid, and asking whether Greece would authorize him to negotiate an exchange on a compulsory basis, including Constantinople. He advised that during the peace negotiations Greece should seek to secure real guarantees for the security and well being of the Greek population of Constantinople and to insert a clause in the peace treaty providing for the non-application of the treaty of compulsory exchange for the Greeks of Constantinople. He was deeply concerned that if the Constantinopolitan Greeks were not covered by treaty, the Turks would force them out and essentially confiscate their property.[51] Nansen also asked Politis to send experts to Constantinople who could negotiate the details of a treaty, once the basic principles were accepted by the parties, speak in the name of the government, and, if necessary, would be authorized to sign an agreement without further delay. It is interesting that in his telegram, Nansen did not inform Athens that Turkey would insist that Western Thrace be excluded from the population exchange.

Two days later, on November 2, Nansen received the reply of the Greek government through its High Commissioner in Constantinople, indicating that it could not accept a population exchange that included the Greek population of Constantinople. Politis made the point of stressing that up to this point there was no mention of that population because "we have always had in mind only the Greek population of Asia Minor and Thrace where forced emigration was already a *fait accompli*."[52] He emphasized that all Greece wanted was the departure of those Greeks remaining in Anatolia, whose families had already emigrated, and the emigration from Greece of the Muslim population, whose houses were necessary, "*par une juste recipro-*

---

[51] *Nansen Papers*, R 1761 (1922), 48/24318/24318, Nansen (Constantinople) to Politis (Athens). October 31, 1922; an*d AYE*, 1922: 88(2)1,1, Simopoulos (Constantinople) to Politis (Athens), November 1, 1922.

[52] *Nansen Papers*, R 1761 (1922), 48/24318/24318, Greek Ministry of Foreign Affairs to Nansen, November 3, 1922.

*cité,*" to provide shelter for the unfortunate Greek refugees already expelled from Turkey. "It never occurred to our thought," he continued, "that some other Greek population, and especially that of Constantinople, should be obliged to leave their homes. (Il n'a jamais pu entrer dans notre pensée de préposer que d'autres population grecques et spécialement celles de Consple [Constantinople] fussent obligées de quitter leurs foyers). This particular sentence could be viewed as confirmation that Athens had accepted the idea of a compulsory exchange for the Greeks of Anatolia and Thrace but not for "other Greek populations" such as the Greeks of Constantinople. Politis then went on to explain to Nansen that the Greek public would revolt if the government, which was only a provisional one, accepted such a monstrous thing as the uprooting and forced departure of 400,000 Greeks of Constantinople. And that the question had an international character, reflecting on the economic interests of the Great Powers in Constantinople and their heavy dependence on the Greek population of that city. Politis concluded the cable by stating that until a satisfactory accord of principle was reached with Turkey, it appeared to him, at the present time, useless and dangerous to bring together the experts of the two governments, and asked Nansen to proceed with the negotiations for a population exchange, excluding Constantinople. Although clearly implied, nowhere in the Politis response is there a definite acceptance of a compulsory exchange; and thus the issue of compulsion was left open.

On the same day, Nansen replied to Politis that he too "had the conviction that it would be impossible to negotiate an accord between the governments of Greece and Turkey on the basis of a forced exchange of populations including the city of Constantinople;" and that he was relieved and happy to note that the Greek government shared his opinion on the subject. The Allied High Commissioners in Constantinople had agreed with him that it would be impossible to negotiate with the Turks if they insisted on including the Greeks of Constantinople in the exchange.[53] On November 4,

---

[53] *Ibid.* and *AYE*, 1922: 88(2)1,1, Nansen (Constantinople) to Politis (Athens), November 3, 1922.

Nansen advised Drummond in Geneva that he did not feel free to negotiate a population exchange if it included the expulsion of the Greek population from Constantinople.[54] He also informed Venizelos of developments in Constantinople and of his relief that the Greek government categorically refused to include the Constantinopolitan Greeks in the compulsory exchange of populations.[55] Venizelos' response was that he too would not accept a compulsory population exchange if it included Constantinople.[56] Earlier, he had informed Politis of his opposition to the eviction of the Greeks of Constantinople, arguing essentially that if it took place it would be extremely difficult to absorb them on top of the million refugees currently in Greece. Even with the eviction of all the Turks [including those in Western Thrace], there would be no relief for Greece because their total number hardly exceeds those of the Greeks of Constantinople and vicinity alone.

### Nansen's Last Bid for Negotiations with Angora

Nansen was, not surprisingly, perplexed and frustrated by Turkey's apparent dilatory tactics which appeared aimed at foiling a serious agreement. He complained that he did not mind the fighting but that the waiting was getting to him. "It can drive me mad."[57] Not being allowed to negotiate with the Angora government but having three separate assurances from it that it was in principle agreeable to a population exchange, Nansen decided on one last ditch effort to move the negotiation process forward. On November 2, he sent a memorandum, through Hamid, to the Angora government, explaining his desire to obtain a solution to the questions which kept him so long at Constantinople and that it was impossible for him to remain there much longer. However, in spite of the considerable demands on his

---

[54]*Nansen Papers*, R 1761 (1922), 48/24318/24318, Nansen (Constantinople) to Drummond (Geneva), November 3, 1922.
[55]*Ibid.*, Nansen (Constantinople) for Venizelos (Athens), November 4, 1922.
[56]*Ibid.*, Venizelos (Paris) to Nansen (Constantinople), November 4, 1922.
[57]Huntford, *Nansen*, p. 527.

schedule, he let it be known that he was willing to remain in the city for a limited time if the information given him by the Turkish government seemed to offer any possibility of reaching a solution. To this end, Nansen invited the Angora government to respond to three questions, expressing the hope of a reply by November 6:

1. Is the Angora Government prepared to negotiate without delay, and independently of the Peace negotiations, an agreement for the exchange of populations on the principle of a voluntary emigration of the racial minorities in Turkey and Greece?

2. Is the Angora Government prepared to appoint delegates with full powers to conclude with Greek representatives, and under my auspices, an agreement which would be submitted immediately for ratification by the two Governments?

3. Does the Angora Government accept that the male refugees deported in Asia Minor will be included in the population exchange?[58]

Nansen also asked for a separate reply as to whether the Angora government was willing to negotiate for an immediate exchange of prisoners of war and civil hostages. He wished to treat this matter apart from the exchange of populations. He also sent Angora a detailed draft treaty drawn up with the help of his aides who had served on the Greek-Bulgarian voluntary population exchange commission. Although Nansen went along with their advice that the principle of voluntary emigration was the only safe one, he had some reservations. Nansen was not quite certain, given the very critical situation in Greece, that a system of compulsory emigration might not be necessary nor possibly even desirable, provided that it had the full consent and cooperation, of both the Turkish and Greek governments.[59]

[58]*Ibid.* Nansen (Constantinople) to British High Commissioner Rumbold. November 3, 1922. Nansen also wrote to the French High Commissioner Pellé informing him of his memorandum to Angora and asking him to telegraph the French representative in Angora if "he would give his precious support in order to quickly obtain a favorable response." *Ibid.*, November 2, 1922.

[59]*Nansen Papers*, R 1761 (1922), 48/24722/24357, A supplementary note by Dr. Nansen

On the following day, Nansen was called to Athens on urgent business relating to refugee relief. Having been informed that there was no boat to Athens between the 4th and 8th of November from Constantinople, he decided in order not to lose time to leave for Athens on November 4. Prior to his departure, Nansen sent the following letter to Hamid:

Your Excellency:

With reference to our correspondence and our previous conversations on the subject of an exchange of population between Greece and Turkey, and finally my note with memorandum of November 2*nd*, I have the honour to inform you that I find it necessary to consult the Greek authorities on various questions. I feel bound to take advantage of the departure of a boat for Athens this afternoon, otherwise I shall not have an opportunity of leaving until Wednesday next. In this way, I shall be free to continue, without loss of time, the negotiations already begun between us. I beg you to be good enough to send me any communications from the Government of the Turkish Grand National Assembly to my office here. . . . I have given instructions . . . that any communication from you or from your substitute at Constantinople shall be telegraphed to me, or if necessary sent to me by wireless in order that I may be informed without delay, and so be able to take the steps which such communication mar require.[60]

Although Nansen had been notified by Athens that there could be no agreement on a population exchange if it included Constantinople, he saw fit to withhold this information from Hamid. He reasoned that it was unwise and unproductive to inform Hamid of the response from Politis since he had not yet received the reply to a similar question submitted to Angora.

While in Athens, Nansen had touched on many issues pertaining to the refugees and their settlement in Greece. It was then that he first

attached to his report concerning the points to be submitted for consideration by the Lausanne conference (Geneva), November 15, 1922.

[60] *Nansen Papers,* R 1761 (1922), 48/24318/24318, Letter of Nansen to Hamid, Constantinople, November 4, 1922.

explained in some detail to the Greek government the possibility of negotiating with the Council of the League of Nations an international loan for refugee resettlement,[61] anticipating the role that would be played by international financial institutions a quarter of a century later.[62] He remained in the Greek capital until November 9, without knowing if his last communication was received by the Nationalist authorities. The silence from Angora and the news of Hamid's sudden departure for Switzerland brought the negotiations to an end. A disappointed Nansen left for Geneva, determined more than ever to bring to a successful conclusion his struggle on behalf of the refugees and to secure for them a much needed international loan necessary for their survival.

How does one explain the evasive and dilatory tactics that were clearly adopted by the Angora government in its dealing with Nansen? One can accept the Turkish position that "it did not consider the issues [posed by Nansen] to have a character of urgency and that its examination could wait after the conclusion of peace." For Angora, there were certainly more profound and pressing issues of a military and political character to command its immediate attention. Or one could argue that the Turkish authorities wished to postpone a binding decision on the question of population exchange until after they completed their policy of getting rid of as many Ottoman Greeks as possible before the conclusion of peace.[63] According to Svolopoulos, the elimination of Hellenism in Anatolia before the conclusion of peace would strengthen Turkey's diplomatic position, which would have the possibility either to negotiate the principle of the population exchange on the basis of the removal of the Greeks from Constantinople, or by refusing an exchange, to compel Greece to keep its Turks with established minority rights.[64]

---

[61]Clouzot, "La Société des Nations et les secours dans le Proche Orient," p. 978.

[62]Such as the Marshall Plan, the IMF, the World Bank, and other aid mechanisms created by the United Nations and by the European Union.

[63]Great Britain, Public Record Office (PRO), FO 371/7860 [E 13187], *Turkey.* Henderson (Constantinople) to Foreign Office (London), November 26, 1922.

[64]Svolopoulos, *I apofasi gia tin ypohreotiki andalagi ton plithismon metaxi Ellados kai Tourkias*, p. 22.

One can also advance the thesis that the refusal of the Turkish government to deal with Nansen on a wide range of issues—from refugee relief and a population exchange to the release of detainees, prisoners of war and civilian hostages—was part and parcel of its military and political strategy to undermine the Greek state. Such action was deemed necessary by Angora because the renewal of hostilities with Greece over territorial and financial matters (Turkey's demand for reparations) was a very real possibility, at least until an agreement on a Near East peace was secured at Lausanne. The Turkish leadership also understood that an ineffective Greece at Lausanne would help strengthen its position at the negotiating table with the Allied Powers.

Angora's treatment of Nansen can also be explained by the fact that no official relations existed between Turkey and the League of Nations. The Angora government refused to participate in the talks Nansen attempted to initiate, seeking to restrain the widening of his activities because it regarded him as a private individual.[65] Essentially, the talks failed because Turkey, whose consent was crucial, did not want them to succeed, at least not until the conclusion of the peace conference. And, indeed, it was Nansen's doggedness and determination that they succeed as soon as possible, his efforts to get the Turks to do something they did not want to do at that time, that led them to tell the French that Nansen had not been tactful in conducting his now abortive negotiations with Angora and that he was much disliked by the Turks.[66] This was not the first time, nor would it be the last, that for his repeated appeals and determined efforts on behalf of the aggrieved and downtrodden (he seldom took no for an answer), Nansen would be labeled obnoxious, arrogant, or simply naive.

---

[65]K. Koufa and C. Svolopoulos, "The Compulsory Exchange of Populations between Greece and Turkey," p. 279.

[66]DBFP, XVIII, Doc. 196, Hardinge (Paris) to Curzon (London), November 15, 1922. Perhaps they recalled that it was Nansen, as the Norwegian delegate, at the First Assembly of the League in 1920, who asked that 60,000 soldiers be sent at once to the Near East to save the Armenians from extermination by the Kemalists. Nansen also broached the issue of the Armenians at the Second and Third Assemblies. Reynolds, Nansen, p. 253.

The Lausanne conference did not start its proceedings on the Greek refugee crisis and related issues from scratch. The work of Nansen and his staff on the question of a population exchange, on the issues of the detainees and the exchange of prisoners of war and civil hostages, were to serve as important guidelines at the conference, including the principle that Nansen had established that an accord on the population exchange be reached without delay and independent of the peace negotiations. Circulated among the Lausanne participants were the series of reports by Nansen and his staff on the above questions, and a preliminary draft accord presenting their views relative to a voluntary population exchange between Greece and Turkey, which served as a blueprint for the Greek-Turkish population exchange agreement signed at Lausanne on January 31, 1923. Moreover, practically all of the participants at Lausanne, including the British, French, and Italian High Commissioners in Constantinople who served as advisors to their respective national delegations, were not only intimately aware of Nansen's efforts to resolve the Greek refugee question but were clearly supportive of those efforts.

PART II

# Fridtjof Nansen
# The Peace Conference of
# Lausanne and After

# CHAPTER IV

# The Compulsory Exchange of Populations Agreement, January 30, 1923

The conclusion of the armistice of Mudanya, which became operative on October 15, 1922, opened the way for the peace conference at Lausanne. The Turkish delegation had already left by train for Switzerland, expecting the conference to open on November 13,[1] only to learn that it had been rescheduled to meet a week later on November 20. This intensified Turkish fears that Britain was deliberately delaying the opening of the conference, using the extra time to forge an Allied united front, at Turkey's expense. While there were legitimate reasons for this postponement, it is also true that Curzon used the extra time to fashion an agreement with Italy and France on the fundamental principles that were to guide the discussions at Lausanne.[2]

With much fanfare, the first plenary meeting of the conference was held in a large hall at the grand but worn out Hotel de Château at Ouchy on the shores of Lake Geneva. There the makers of the new Europe crowded to set the borders of a victorious Turkey and to

---

[1]On October 18, the Allies had agreed that the site of the conference would be Lausanne. It seems that the peace conference was originally scheduled to open on November 1, but at Curzon's request, it was rescheduled for November 13, "as the earliest practical date in all circumstances." The request seemed legitimate, in that the delegations required more time to make hotel arrangements and other accommodations and because of the uncertainty of the internal political situation in Britain and Italy. Curzon then informed Pioncaré "that we should announce a date as soon as possible to appease Angora." *DBFP*, XVIII, Doc. 127. Curzon (London) to Pioncaré (Paris), October 18, 1922. On the following day, the Conservative party left the British war-time coalition government, compelling Lloyd George to resign. In Italy, there was a change of government, and Mussolini signaled his intention to head the Italian delegation at Lausanne.

[2]This agreement was reached on November 18. Harold Nicolson, *Curzon: The Last Phase, 1919–1925; a Study in Post-war Diplomacy* (London: Constable, 1937), pp. 282–287; Henry H. Cumming, *Franco-British Rivalry in the Post-War Near East: The Decline of French Influence* (London: Oxford University Press, 1938), p. 189; and *DDI*, Series 7, Vol. 1, Doc. 125.

decide the fate of a defeated Greece. The first business meeting of the conference began on the following day, November 21, with Curzon in the chair, establishing rules and procedures. Three principal commissions were appointed to deal with: (1) territorial and military questions, chairman Curzon; (2) regime of foreigners and minorities in Turkey, chairman Garroni; and (3) financial and economic questions, ports and railways, health arrangements, chairman Barrère. The actual work of the conference began on November 22, when the Territorial and Military Commission, with Curzon at the chair, opened with a discussion of Western Thrace.[3]

The question of Western Thrace was high on both the Turkish and Greek agendas and directly related to the question of the population exchange. Ismet, Turkey's chief delegate at Lausanne, demanded that the border of Eastern Thrace revert to that of 1913,[4] and that a plebiscite be held in Western Thrace to determine its future status. Both claims were unanimously rejected because Turkey was not a party to the 1919 Neuilly treaty by which Bulgaria ceded Western

---

[3]For the proceedings at Lausanne, see Great Britain, *Parliamentary Papers, 1923, Turkey,* No. 1, Cmd., 1814, "Lausanne Conference on Near Eastern Affairs, 1922–1923" (Proceedings), London 1923. Hereafter cited as LCNEA. For the question of Thrace, see also Psomiades, *The Eastern Question,* Chapter V, "The Struggle for Thrace."

[4]A Turkish note to the Allies of September 29 and October 4 had called for a Greek withdrawal to the west bank of the Evros or Maritsa river, and the Allies agreed. They referred to it as the 1914 line. But there were only two officially recognized boundaries: that of 1913, whereby Turkey regained from Bulgaria in the Second Balkan War much of Thrace extending several kilometers into the region on the west bank of the Evros; and that of 1915, when Turkey, in order to entice Bulgaria to enter the world war on the side of the Central Powers, ceded to Bulgaria a strip of territory on both sides of the Evros river, thus providing Bulgaria with a potential port and outlet to the Aegean. In 1919, in the Treaty of Neuilly with Bulgaria, Greece acquired Western Thrace up to the 1915 line. At Mudanya, the Greeks insisted that the border between Western and Eastern Thrace was the 1915 line and that they should not have to withdraw their forces to the west bank of the Evros. They insisted, in part, on the official 1915 line for fear if they did not do so, they would be pushed back to the 1913 line, which included all of Didimoticho, with its substantial Greek population. They also did not want to give up territory which was theirs by virtue of the Neuilly treaty, an international recognized instrument. At Lausanne, the Turks were to express their regrets that they did not demand the 1913 line at Mudanya. By being on the west bank of the Evros they believed that they could have exerted greater pressure to force a plebiscite in Western Thrace and deprive the Greeks of a military advantage by denying it the high ground on the west bank of the river. At Lausanne, the Turkish claim for the 1913 border was denied by the Allies, although they did offer a small enclave between the 1915 boundary and the Evros. For a detailed discussion, see Psomiades, *Eastern Thrace and the Armistice of Mudanya,* pp. 1–67.

Thrace to Greece and because at Mudanya the Turks had accepted the Evros or Maritsa river as their new Thracian boundary with Greece. For the Allies at Mudanya, the Evros was a natural geographic divide between the two states. In any case, by pushing the Greek population of Eastern Thrace into Western Thrace, the Nationalists undermined their own claim for a plebiscite in a province that by now had a significant Greek majority. During the debate, Venizelos admitted that the Greek element in Western Thrace increased with the influx of the Greek refugees from Eastern Thrace. "If the Greek majority has become a large majority because of the influx of these refugees you cannot blame it on Greece or that Greece deliberately provoked the change." The Greeks of Eastern Thrace left their homes "because they knew once the Turks arrived their presence would not be tolerated. . . . They would be compelled to leave their homes as their brothers in Asia Minor have been forced to leave."[5]

Ismet was charged by his government not to concede anything contrary to the National Pact of January 28, 1920, which *inter alia* called for a plebiscite in Western Thrace.[6] It may be that Ismet put up a good fight at Lausanne on a losing issue to placate the nationalists and hotheads who, after the Greek defeat, wanted to take the war to all of Thrace. It also may explain why in the Turkish discussions with Nansen, Angora insisted that the projected compulsory exchange of populations exempt the Muslims of Western Thrace.

Meanwhile, during the first week of discussions at Lausanne on territorial issues, there were disturbing reports that with the approach of winter the Turks were continuing their war time policy of evicting the Greeks and Armenians from their homes and driving them to the Black Sea ports. On November 26, both the French and

[5] *AMAE,* Vol. 317. Conference of Lausanne, First Session, Territorial and Military Committee, November 22, 1922, pp. 20–21.

[6] Paragraph 3 of the National Pact:" The determination of the juridical status of Western Thrace, which has been made dependent on the Turkish peace, must be effected in accordance with the votes which shall be given the inhabitants in complete freedom." For details, see Psomiades, *Eastern Thrace and the Armistice of Mudanya,* pp. 39–40; see also *AMAE,* Vol. 155, Memorandum from Pellé (Constantinople) to the French Ministry of Foreign Affairs, November 21, 1922, reporting on the guidelines or restraints placed upon Ismet by Angora at Lausanne.

British High Commissioners in Constantinople wired their representatives at Lausanne that all Christians in Anatolia have been informed by the Turkish authorities that they are free to leave the country, except for the able bodied men ages 16–50, who will be placed in the infamous labor battalions. But they must leave before November 30 and in some cases before December 15. "Those who do not leave by the fixed dates are given to understand that they will be deported to internment camps in the interior. Panic methods appear to be fully successful and my latest information is that roads to Ineboli and Samsun [Black Sea ports] are crowded with refugees. . . . Whether it is called expulsion or permission to depart, object of Turks and result is identical. . . . The aim of Angora is to get rid of as many as possible before the conclusion of peace."[7] On December 29, Venizelos asked Curzon to tell the Turks, on humanitarian grounds, to stop the deportation of masses of Greeks in the middle of winter. The Turks were violating the agreement that the exchange would not take place until May 1923.[8]

These developments did not escape Nansen's attention. Two days later, he informed Venizelos that there were 20,000 destitute refugees in Samsun alone, barely kept alive by the American Near East Relief and waiting for transportation to Greece. The ever pragmatic Nansen told Venizelos that since Greek ships were not allowed in Turkish waters, he had made arrangements for British ships to pick up the refugees, provided that the Greek government pay the difference between the cost of a British ship in Constantinople and the cost of sending it to Samsun. He also asked if the Greek government would sent ships to Constantinople to pick up another 5,000 refugees.[9] At

---

[7] PRO FO 371/7960, E13187, Henderson (Constantinople) to Curzon (Lausanne), November 26, 1922.

[8] *AYE*, 1923:2(2)3,2. Venizelos (Lausanne) to Curzon (Lausanne), December 29, 1922.

[9] *Venizelos Papers*, 173/318, Nansen (Lausanne) and Venizelos (Lausanne), November 28, 1922. On December 2, 1922, the United States promised to give unofficial protection to have Greek boats go to the Black Sea ports without flying the Greek colors. *Nansen Papers*, R 1761 (1922), 48/24938/24938. "Transportation of Refugees." But this was soon rescinded by Washington, stating that those at Lausanne should take action with the government of Angora to allow Greek ships into the Black Sea. *Venizelos Papers*, 33, Kanellopoulos (Constantinople) to Athens ands a copy to Venizelos at Lausanne, December 6, 1922.

the same time, the captain of an American destroyer dispatched to the harbors of the Pontos telegraphed from Samsun that he found abandoned and in poor condition some 20,000 refugees on the road between Sivas and Samsun.[10] Even Ismet felt compelled to complain to Angora that the evictions should cease because they harm the Turkish position at Lausanne.[11] But his complaint was ignored.

## Nansen's Testimony at Lausanne

It was not until the 8th meeting of the Territorial and Military Commission, on December 1, that the issues which Nansen had been grappling with in Greece and Turkey came up for discussion at Lausanne. The agenda for that afternoon was the exchange of prisoners and populations. In his opening remarks, Curzon told the commission that it should first discuss a question of immediate importance arising directly out of the exchange of prisoners of war, namely the exchange of populations between Greek and Turkish territory. For this purpose, he had invited Dr. Nansen, who had for some time been in negotiation with Greece and Turkey on the question of population exchange, to present his views on the subject. Copies of Nansen's testimony, in English, had been communicated to the Greek and Turkish delegations in advance in order to save time. Because Nansen was an unofficial guest, he was barred from speaking himself by the objections of the Turkish delegation that Nansen's mandate was from the League of Nations, with which it had no official relations. Curzon proposed to have the speech read out in French by the interpreter and then to ask for the views of the member of the commission on the subject of population exchange. He hoped "that the discussion would eventuate in something tangible being done."[12] Nansen and his assistant Baker were present at the reading.

---

[10] *Ibid.*

[11] *AYE,* 1922: 8(6)1,1. Ismet(Lausanne) to Rauf (Angora), November 25, 1922. Secret Intercepts; also Yildirim, *Diplomats and Refugees,* p.107; and *Venizelos Papers,* 34, Anninos (Constantinople) to Athens and Lausanne, December 23, 1922.

[12] *LCNEA,* p.113.

Nansen's testimony was not of course a revelation to the participants of the peace conference, who had been apprised of his work
and thoughts for some time.[13] It was rather Nansen's presence that
gave the Greek refugee crisis the sense of urgency that it deserved. In
his report, Nansen gave a brief overview of his negotiations for a populations exchange with the governments of Greece, Turkey, and the
Great Powers and detailed the immense difficulties involved in an
exchange of historic proportions and the very considerable hard-
ships that it would impose on the displaced populations. However,
taking the negatives into consideration, Nansen expressed the belief
that the reasons which made an exchange desirable were of greater
force. To do nothing was not an option. He urged the commission to
act without delay and gave the reasons for doing so.

[13]See, for example, Nansen's widely circulated report of November 18, 1922. *Nansen
Papers*, R 1761 (1922), 48/24722/24357. "Note by Dr. Nansen, supplementary to his report
concerning the points to be submitted for consideration by the Lausanne Conference." The
report began with the heading 1. Exchange of Populations. It called for (a) an immediate
exchange of populations before the conclusion of the general peace in time for the spring
planting; and essential for both parties is the rapid evacuation of the Muslims from Greece.
(b) Constantinople should be excluded from the exchange with really effective guarantees
by the Turks for the minorities who will remain. "At the moment no minority has a belief in
Turkish guarantees." And (c) the draft treaty submitted is based on a voluntary emigration.
But given the critical situation in the Near East "I am not sure that a system of compulsory
emigration may not be necessary and possibly even desirable, provided it has the full consent and cooperation of Greece and Turkey." II. Restoration of Able Bodied Refugees. About
100,000 are retained by the Turks. They must allow them soon to be restored to join their
families, who have already left the country. Greek government has agreed to give assurances
that they will not be drafted by the military. The Turks must recede from their uncompromising stance on this issue. III. Exchanges of Prisoners of War. Should be dealt with immediately; at least initially an equal number should be released on both sides. To achieve this
Greeks have agreed to release some 3,800 civil hostages taken in Asia Minor. IV. Fresh Exodus of Christian Population from Asia Minor. I believe that an additional 300,000–400,000
Christians will be forced to leave Asia Minor by the Turks. I know of no way the exodus can
be prevented, except by impressing on the Turkish delegation here [Lausanne] the very
painful impression that this would cause on the rest of the world if such an exodus takes
place two months after the conclusion of the armistice between the two belligerents. The
report concludes that if things get worse, Greece will need the support of the Powers and an
international loan to deal with the problem. "If the Turkish authorities are allowed to drive
more hundreds of thousands of refugees from their homes and to throw them upon Europe
for their support, during the coming winter, and indeed for an indefinite future, I think that
the Greek Government will have an absolute claim for the assistance of other powers in dealing with the new and appalling problem which will be created and the main burden of which
will mainly fall upon Greece."

He said that since the Great Powers, Greece and Turkey had all agreed that a population exchange was desirable (to unmix the populations of the Near East will secure the true pacification of the Near East), there remained several important political questions that had to be answered before an exchange agreement could be made:[14] (1) whether the agreement should be based on the principle of compulsory or of voluntary emigration, (2) what would be the area of its application, and (3) what is to be the nature of the Mixed Commission or other machinery that by necessity must be established to carry the exchange into its practical execution.

Nansen's message, in brief, was that because the expulsion of the Greeks from Anatolia was irreversible (the Turks would never allow them to return to their homes), it must be regulated by international treaty, providing for the transfer of Muslims from Greece to Turkey to make housing and land available for the massive number of refugees overwhelming Greece.

Ismet's response was to insist that before addressing the question of a population exchange the commission must first resolve the question of the prisoners of war and civil hostages. The Turkish prisoners of war and civil hostages held by Greece ought to be released immediately, while those of Greece would only be released after the signature of peace. The Turkish delegate also added that in his opinion an exchange of population agreement, to be successful, must include the Greek population of Constantinople.[15] After much debate and disagreement, the commission took up the suggestion of Venizelos that a small subcommission should be set up to deal with these issues. The commission then adopted the following resolution:

---

[14] *Ibid.*,pp.113–117. See also *AMAE*, Vol. 156, Telegram of Bompard and Barrère to the French Ministry of Foreign Affairs, December 1, 1922.

[15] Nansen's call for a Greek population exchange brought a sigh of relief to the Turkish delegation. In his memoirs, the Turkish delegate to Lausanne, Riza Nour, wrote " . . . We had wanted to put the population exchange forward but did not dare to do so, hence the delight of the Turkish camp when Nansen grasped the nettle first." Clark, *Twice a Stranger*, p. 94; and Riza Nour, *Hayat ve Hatıratım* [My life and memories] (Istanbul: Garanti Matbaasi, 1967).

It is decided that the question of the exchange of populations between Greece and Turkey, including the return of the prisoners of war and civil hostages, shall be examined by a subcommission consisting of the representatives of each of the inviting Powers, of Turkey and of Greece, under the chairmanship of an Italian delegate [Montagna]. The subcommission will hear Dr. Nansen on the question, and collect such evidence as it may think fit.[16]

The subcommission was immediately formed. On the following day, December 2, it held its first meeting, which was devoted almost entirely to a full oral presentation by Nansen on the results of his investigations in Greece and Turkey and of his suggestions for the speediest possible solution of the issues before the commission. In dispassionate tones he described the deplorable condition of the million Greek refugees and with much reluctance recommended a compulsory population exchange, "the necessity of which arose from grave and exceptional circumstances."[17]

Having presented his views to the commission, Nansen left for Norway on the next day. And a week later, on December 10, he was presented with the Nobel Peace Prize for 1922, not only for his work on the displaced victims of World War I and his assistance for prisoners of war and famine victims in Russia but also for his work with the refugees from Asia Minor and Thrace. True to his character, Nansen donated the prize money, some 80,000 kronors, to assist refugees in Greece, Armenia and Russia.

Meanwhile, the subcommission proceeded to discuss the questions posed by its mandate. On January 8, 1923, after much debate, and notwithstanding sharp disagreement on certain points between the Greek and Turkish delegates, Montagna reported to Curzon the results of the subcommission's work. On the advice of Nansen and at

---

[16]*LCNEA*, pp.123–124.

[17]Several weeks later, Nansen denied that he had proposed a compulsory exchange and that he only explained to the subcommission that a question to be settled was whether the exchange should be voluntary or compulsory, and that this was a matter for the two interested governments alone to decide. PRO, FO 371/9092, E 1431/4/44, "Report on Refugees in the Near east by Dr. Nansen, High Commissioner of the League for Refugees." January 26, 1923.

the insistence of the Allied delegates, the Greek delegation had agreed to release the Turkish civilian hostages as soon as possible. On the question of prisoners of war, it was agreed by mutual consent that Greece would release, at an early date, all of the Turkish prisoners of war and that Turkey would return an equal number of Greek prisoners of war, but that the remainder of the more numerous Greek prisoners in Turkish hands would be returned to Greece only after the conclusion of peace. It was estimated that there were approximately 10,000 Turkish and 25,000–30,000 Greek prisoners of war.

On the question of the population exchange, Montagna reported that all of the delegates of subcommission appeared to admit, albeit reluctantly, the necessity for a compulsory exchange. However, in the course of the discussions, the question of a compulsory exchange was again raised by a written declaration of the Greek delegation that the exchange should be voluntary. "The Turkish delegation definitely opposed this proposal so that the decision previously reached was adhered to … unless it is thought desirable to re-open the question, the exchange of populations would remain compulsory." A first step in the exchange, would be the release of the male hostages who were interned by Turkey during the Greek exodus from Asia Minor and separated from their families. Nansen's recommendation, and the pleas of the Greek delegation that the internees be released immediately to assist in the resettlement of the refugees, were vetoed by the Turkish delegation.

The major stumbling block came with Turkey's demand that the Greek population of Constantinople be included in the compulsory exchange, along with the removal of the Ecumenical Patriarchate. After fierce and acrimonious debate, and confronted with the united opposition of Greece and the Allied Powers, the Turkish delegation relented and agreed that the Greeks of Constantinople be excluded from the exchange, with the exception of those who had migrated to Constantinople since October 30, 1918. But it remained immovable in regard to the removal of the Ecumenical Patriarchate.[18] Therefore, that issue was left to the plenary commission to resolve.

[18]LCNEA, pp. 328–337.

*The Final Stages of the Negotiations*

On January 10, 1923, the Territorial and Military Commission met to hear the report of Montagna. Curzon, as president of the commission, took the initiative in formulating a solution of the problem of the Ecumenical Patriarchate. With the unanimous support of the inviting powers and of the Orthodox Christian states of the commission, he met the Turkish demand for the removal of the Patriarchate with equal firmness. Curzon took up the French and Greek recommendations in the subcommission's report, whereby the Patriarchate would remain in Constantinople on the condition that it give up the political power bestowed upon it by the defunct Ottoman state. He declared that he saw no reason why the Patriarchate should not continue to exercise its spiritual and ecclesiastical prerogatives without enjoying any sort of political and administrative authority. Venizelos also urged Ismet to accept Curzon's proposals for the retention of the Patriarchate in its historical seat and declared that if they were accepted, the Greek delegation would "take steps with a view to the retirement of the Patriarch now in power."[19] But Ismet would not yield. For almost two weeks the issue of the Patriarchate threatened to provoke a complete rupture of the negotiations. Finally, on January 28, Ismet relented and stated that Turkey, "taking note of the solemn declarations and assurances which have just been given concerning the future situation and attitude of the Patriarchate and in order to give a supreme proof of its conciliatory dispositions, renounces the expulsion of the Patriarchate from Constantinople."[20] The door was now open for the conclusion of the negotiations and

---

[19]*LCNEA*, pp.324–325; and Harold Nicolson, *Curzon*, p. 320. Meletios IV, who had been the Ecumenical Patriarch since December 1921, was understandably a *persona non grata* to the Turkish government because of his anti-Turkish activities. While the Turkish government was calling for the removal of the Ecumenical Patriarchate from Turkey at Lausanne, at home it sought to undermine that institution by supporting for a while the Turkish Orthodox Church plan of Papa Efthim Karahissarides to replace the Greek Patriarchate. For details see Psomiades, *The Eastern Question*, pp. 91–97.

[20]*AMAE*, "Conference de Lausanne," I, Paris 1923, p. 268. It was a verbal agreement inserted in the verbatim proceedings and does not appear in any article in the exchange agreement, nor in the Lausanne treaty. While verbal agreements are arguably binding under international law, Turkey maintained then, and to this day, that the position of the Patriar-

for the signature of a convention concerning the compulsory exchange of Greek and Turkish populations on January 30, 1923. In short, the convention ratified the exodus of the Greek population from Asia Minor, Pontos, and Eastern Thrace and regulated the forthcoming expulsions of the Muslims from Greece. The exceptions to the exchange were the Muslims of Western Thrace and the Greeks of Constantinople. The exchange convention was to come into force only with the ratification of the Lausanne treaty of peace.

The convention closely followed Nansen's proposals, especially those for the creation of a Mixed Commission (Article 11), whose duties were to supervise and facilitate the emigration and to carry out the liquidation of the movable and immovable property of the exchanged persons. Both the Mixed Commission and its subcommissions were to include Greek and Turkish members, but the president of the Commission and each subcommission was to be chosen by the Council of the League of Nations from among the nationals of Powers that did not take part in the war of 1914–1918.[21] Because the peace treaty of Lausanne was not signed until July 23, 1923, and ratified the following month, the exchange of populations was delayed by agreement until May 1, 1924. Nevertheless, several thousands of Greeks and Turks were transferred under the supervision of the Mixed Commission, with the approval of the two governments, throughout 1923 and 1924. From 1923 to 1925, over 180,000 Greeks and 355,000 Muslims were transferred under the auspices of the Mixed Commission.[22] Nansen, as the League's High Commissioner for Refugees, was to play a major role in the care and particularly in

chate is not governed by international law. "It could not be otherwise since Turkey would not accept a document or an international engagement relative to a question of a purely domestic nature." Speech on February 4, 1925 by the Turkish Prime Minister, Fethi (Okyar), delivered to the Turkish Grand National Assembly, France, Ministère des Affaires Étrangères, *Bulletin périodique de la presse turque*, Paris, No. 39, April 21, 1925.

[21]See Appendix II.

[22]Psomiades, *The Eastern Question*, pp. 67–68. The liquidation of such vast properties by the Mixed Commission proved to be an extremely difficult task. The Mixed Commission all too frequently could not agree on the value of the property and on a plan to indemnify the refugees, and in the end, Greece and Turkey agreed that the only solution for compensation to the refugees was by direct negotiations. The impasse was finally overcome by the Convention of Ankara, June 10, 1930. *Ibid.*, pp. 81–83.

the actual transportation of the refugees to their respective "mother-lands."

## The Blame Game

Much of the discussion at Lausanne was taken up with the question concerning the legitimacy and morality of the obligatory nature of the exchange. Because all of the delegates vigorously condemned the principle of a compulsory exchange, which they all found repugnant, but nevertheless signed off on, they all rejected its paternity. Each accused the other of initiating the idea of compulsion, with Veniza-los and Nansen given most of the blame. Ismet felt obliged to say that it was his impression that the compulsory exchange was proposed and supported in the negotiations by the Greek delegation. An alle-gation immediately refuted by Venizelos, who declared that Greece would abandon the entire idea of an exchange on the condition that Turkey would permit the expelled refugees to return to their homes. The response by Ismet and by the inviting Powers was a complete silence, implying that the decision was irreversible.[23] Nansen accused the inviting Powers of fostering the exchange when their High Com-missioners in Constantinople had invited him to proceed along the lines of a compulsory exchange. Rumbold of the British delegation replied that, on the contrary, it was Nansen who first introduced that idea of a compulsory exchange when he came to the meeting of the High Commissioners, a meeting at which he was present. In brief, Venizelos and Nansen both agreed with the proposition of Turkey and of the inviting Powers for an obligatory exchange, primarily because of Turkish actions and statements, which ruled out any other alternative. The idea of a population exchange is to be found by implication in Nansen's letter of October 10 and, more directly, in his subsequent statements. Clearly in Venizelos' letters of October 13 and 17, the paternity of the idea of a *compulsory* exchange first came from

---

[23]It was only through the mediation of Curzon that Venizelos relented and accepted the principle of compulsion. Douglas Dakin, *The Unification of Greece, 1770–1923* (London: E. Benn, 1972), p. 243. Dakin was the editor of volume XVIII, *DBFP.*

Hamid, speaking on behalf of his government and insisting upon an *échange obligatoire*.[24] From Hamid's statement of November 1 and all subsequent statements by Angora and by its representatives at Lausanne, an exchange accord could only be on the basis of an integral and obligatory exchange of populations.[25]

---

[24]See Hamid's statement in Constantinople to Nansen on November 1, 1922.

[25]Although the issue of the population exchange was to be resolved independently of the peace negotiations at Lausanne, it was directly affected by the course of those negotiations. For the disagreements of the various delegations (Britain over Mosul and France on economic issues) and, in particular, the disagreements between Greece and Turkey over other issues, such as the Turkish demand that Greece pay reparations, which had seriously threatened the halt negotiations and the denunciation of the Mudanya armistice, and thus making the population exchange agreement null and void, see Psomiades, *The Eastern Question*.

# CHAPTER V

# Nansen: The Last Phase, 1923–1930

The population exchange agreement was one thing; to provide for the permanent settlement of the refugees was quite a different matter. From the very beginning of their involvement in the Greek refugee crisis, both Nansen and Venizelos realized that without significant international financial and administrative support for refugee settlement, the refugees would be an unbearable burden in an impoverished and politically turbulent Greek state. As early as October 1922, Nansen had suggested to the Greek government that it seek an international loan for the settlement of the refugees through the instrumentality of the League of Nations. He also proposed that a committee be formed under the aegis of the Minister of Public Assistance, with an executive subcommittee headed by a representative of the League. Its task would be to draw up plans on how the proceeds of the international loan should be spent for refugee settlement.[1] Furthermore, in mid-November 1922, in his detailed report on the Greek refugee crisis, Nansen urged the Council of the League of Nations, with the concurrence of Athens, that it consider, without delay, the need for floating an international loan to finance the settlement and integration of the refugees into the Greek economy.[2] By that time it was clear that the Greek refugees could not return to their former homes.

With the January 1923 compulsory population exchange agreement, the need for an international refugee loan took on a greater urgency. Fortunately, the participation of the Powers in the exchange agreement carried with it an obligation to assist in the resettlement of the refugees in Greece. It also became abundantly clear that such

---

[1]Per Vogt, *Fridtjof Nansen* (Oslo: Dreyer Forlag, 1961), pp. 132–141.
[2]*Nansen Papers,* R 1761 (1922), 48/24722/24357. Report of Dr. Nansen, Part II, "The Question of Refugees in Greece and Asia Minor," Geneva, November 18, 1922.

assistance was not simply a matter of humanitarian solicitude but one which touched upon the vital interests of the Powers in the region and on the moral standing of the infant League of Nations.

At the 11th meeting of the Council of the League on February 2, 1923, Nansen again reported on the desperate situation of the refugees and the need for a substantial international loan for their settlement in Greece. At the same meeting, the Greek representative, Nicholas Politis, following the lead of Nansen, officially acknowledged that his government, given the financial resources at its disposal, could not cope with the refugee problem, and that an international loan of £10 million was absolutely indispensable for their settlement.[3] The Council adopted the proposal of the Greek government and referred the question to the Finance Committee of the League for examination and report. This moved the Financial Committee, and subsequently a subcommittee, to explore the possibility of a loan on the basis of what securities (revenues and assets) could be offered by Greece against the loan.

The question of the loan became a matter of greater urgency when on March 31, 1923, the American Secretary of State, Charles E. Hughes, wrote a letter to the ambassadors of Britain, France, and Italy informing them that the feeding of the great camps of Greek refugees could not and should not continue indefinitely and that the American Red Cross (ARC) will terminate its emergency relief work in Greece on June 30, 1923. In his note he also suggested that some international action should be undertaken to help Greece in whatever manner seemed most necessary. He expressed the view that finding a home for the refugees and absorbing them in the normal economic life of the country would require the cordial cooperation of the local authorities and of the Powers, whose territorial and other interests in the Mediterranean region may make it possible for them to assist.[4] As a result of the positive response of the ambassadors,

---

[3] *LNOJ*, 4th Year, No. 3, (March 1923), Geneva. Appendix 471, "Refugees in the Near East," pp. 234–5, 383–6; and Clausen, *Dr. Fridtjof Nansen's Work*, p. 11.

[4] *Foreign Relations of the United States (FRUS)*, Note of Secretary of State, Charles E. Hughes, to the British, French and Italian Ambassadors in Washington D.C., March 31,

Hughes ordered his representative in Geneva to attend the meetings of the League's Financial Committee in a consultative capacity.

## The Refugee Settlement Commission

In the meantime, Nansen had again informed the Council of the need for a general plan of refugee settlement on a self-supporting basis and of the necessity for the swift termination of emergency aid. Very early on he also saw the futility of continuing with merely philanthropic measures, which could drag on for years, demoralize the refugees, and overtax the world's charities.[5] Consequently, at a meeting held on April 23, 1923, the Council asked Nansen to devise, in consultation with the Greek government, a scheme for refugee settlement. It also appointed a subcommittee, known hereafter as the Greek subcommittee, consisting of the British, French and Italian members of the Council, with authority to invite the Greek government to add a fourth member. The subcommittee would receive the reports of the Finance Committee and advise the Council whether the League could itself properly and usefully accept responsibility for the settlement of the refugees.

As a result of the Council's directives, Nansen and his staff immediately began their investigation into the practicality of a comprehensive solution to the refugee problem.[6] The study was based, in

1923, Washington D.C., 1923, p. 331. See also the *Annual Report of the American National Red Cross for the Year ending June 30, 1923,* Washington D.C. 1923, p. 61; and Charles B. Eddy, *Greece and the Greek Refugees* (London: G. Allen & Unwin, 1931), pp. 56–57.

[5] Between 1915–1922, the United States alone had spent over $82 million on behalf of the Near East refugees, including $11.6 million in 1922. See the letter of C.V. Vickery, Secretary General of the American Near East Relief to Johnson, the League's Assistant Commissioner for Refugees dated June 13, 1923 in *League of Nations,* C 1320, Archives of the Nansen Office, Geneva.

[6] By the time Nansen began the study, considerable progress had been made by the Greek government and the Nansen team in settling 10,000 Greek refugees in Western Thrace. *LNOJ,* 4th Year, No. 6 (June 1923), Annex 515, "Near East Refugees: Western Thrace Refugee Settlement," pp. 696–703. It was the success of this limited program that convinced Nansen that a similar scheme on a much larger scale was doable. Not surprisingly, when the Refugee Settlement Commission was finally established, it saw no need to make an entirely fresh start and preferred to bring under its authority the machinery operating the limited program in Western Thrace. *LNOJ,* 5th Year, No. 4 (April 1924), Annex 610, "Greek Refugees," p. 586.

part, on previous recommendations of the Nansen team that a refugee settlement commission be appointed under the control of the League of Nations not only to administer the funds of an international loan but also to provide the necessary executive duties in connection with the actual planning and spending on each project. It was believed that such control by the League would encourage investors to participate in the international loan for Greece. League control, it was argued, would ensure that the refugee funds were spent wisely in accordance with the settlement scheme and as a consequence improve considerably Greece's financial standing.

Indeed, when in August 1923 action for the Greek loan was facilitated by the offer of the Bank of England to provide a million pounds for refugee settlement purposes, it was on condition, *inter alia,* that a refugee settlement commission, under League control, should be appointed to supervise the loan and settlement work.[7]

In September 1923, such a commission was accordingly organized by the Council of the League, with much input from the Nansen team. It approved a protocol, in agreement with Athens, by which the Greek government undertook to establish a Refugee Settlement Commission (RSC). It conferred on the RSC the responsibilities for refugee settlement, assigned to it the entire proceeds of the loan raised for such purposes, and made available to the RSC over 500,000 hectares of land for refugee projects. The League Council shortly thereafter approved the organic statutes of the RSC, which was to consist of four members: two appointed by the Greek government, with the approval of the Council of the League, one selected by the Council of the League, and a fourth one, its Chairman, who had to be a national of the United States, representing relief organizations. The statutes ensured the autonomy of the RSC and assigned to it extraordinary powers, including the takeover of the local Greek ministries of health and public assistance.[8] The RSC was accountable to the Council of the League, to which it was to submit quarterly

[7]*LNOJ*, 4th Year, No. 8 (August 1923), p. 903

[8]For details see Pentzopoulos, *The Balkan Exchange of Minorities and its Impact upon Greece*, pp. 84–86; and *LNOJ.*, 4th Year, No. 11 (November 1923) Annex 580, pp. 1506–1509.

progress reports. In fact, the League of Nations, following Nansen's lead, had created an autonomous, super-national body, which provided for the first time the administrative framework for the permanent settlement of refugees.

On November 11, 1923, the RSC met for the first time in Thessaloniki, setting in motion its great humanitarian work, with sufficient Greek input to make it acceptable to the Greek authorities. Although the United States contributed to the conception of the RSC, the lead taken by the Nansen team under the auspices of the League of Nations for refugee settlement dealt a fatal blow to all hopes of American participation in its organization. Petty rivalries and personal quarrels aside, the United States eventually declined to participate in a permanent settlement scheme, except for emergency relief, because it did not allow for suitable American supervision. It would have been a different story if the United States Senate had not rejected membership in the League of Nations. On the other hand, the insistence of the League of Nations that the Chairmanship of the RSC be an American went a long way to ensure its success.[9] It wisely appointed as its first Chairman Henry Morgenthau, a man whose sympathies for the Greeks and Armenians were well known but who could also gain the confidence of the international financial community. Morgenthau was a successful lawyer and real estate magnate, a former U.S. ambassador in Constantinople, and a member of the executive committee of the American Near East Relief. His support for the Greek refugee loan could hardly be ignored.[10]

[9]The changes in the highly qualified membership of the RSC were as follows: The American Chairmen were Henry Morgenthau (September 1923–December 1924), Alfred Bonzon as temporary chairman (December 1924–February 1925), Charles P. Howland (February 1925–September 1926), and Charles B. Eddy (October 1926–December 1930). The League representatives were Sir John Campbell (September 1923–January 1927) and Sir John Hope Simpson (January 1927–December 1930). The Greek members were Pericles Argyropoulos (September 1923–August 1924), Etienne Delta (September 1923–August 1925), Theodore Eustathopoulos (August 1924–August 1925), Alexander Pallis and Achilles Lambros (September 1925–December 1930). In December 1930, having settled almost a million refugees, the RSC terminated its work and turned over its responsibilities to the Greek government.

[10]For Morgenthau's effective work as first Chairman of the RSC, see Henry Morgenthau, *I Was Sent to Athens* (New York: Doubleday, Doran & Company, 1929).

*The 1924 Refugee Loan*

Despite the interests of the Powers and the leading role of Nansen and the League of Nations in securing the international loan and in drawing up the prerequisite bylaws of the Refugee Settlement Commission (RSC) which was to administer the loan, it took almost two years before the loan was raised. It was not until December 1924 that Greece signed contracts for a loan of £12,310,000 pounds or $464 million with the Hambros Bank of London (£7.5 million), the Bank of New York (£2.3 million equivalent in dollars) and the National Bank of Greece (£2.5 million). The net proceeds of the loan, which bore the nominal interest of 7%, amounted to about £10 million.[11] For the lenders the real rate was 8%, and the loan was naturally a great success. In fact, it was oversubscribed. These were very onerous terms but could not be otherwise since Greece was clearly viewed by the lenders as a poor risk. Regrettably, more favorable terms were not considered by the financial world despite the fact that the funds were strictly earmarked for the rehabilitation of innocent victims of war.

There were numerous reasons for the delay by the financial community in providing the necessary funds for the RSC to undertake the realization of an epic enterprise. However, it should be kept in mind that regardless of all the hurdles to be overcome, both the League of Nations as an institution and the Powers as political actors had a vested interest in the stability and very survival of the Greek state. Having engineered the compulsory exchange of populations agreement, they had a responsibility for the settlement of its blameless victims. In the case of Britain, there was also Curzon's promise to Venizelos that in return for his major concessions in Eastern Thrace and at Lausanne, Greece would get Allied support for a refugee settlement loan. In the case of the United States, which in the spring of 1923 was still interested in the permanent settlement of the refugees, it was believed that there would be serious repercussions if the loan

---

[11] *League of Nations,* C123, No. 7, "Greek Refugee Loan of 1924," (Geneva), pp. 26–30; and Aretis Tounta-Fergadi, *To prosfygiko daneo tou 1924* [The refugee loan of 1924](Thessaloniki: Parateretes, 1986).

was turned down. Particularly, if there was no bad faith on the part of Greece. The United States and its public, which had contributed millions of dollars for Greek refugee relief, would be outraged.[12] As C.F. Grant, the director of the American Near East Relief wrote at the time, "I personally will hide my face in shame, should we, like the European politicians, desert these refugees in this hour of need."[13] Another major critical factor in support of the loan was Nansen's personal influence and his highly original suggestion of raising the loan with the refugees themselves as security and the Greek state as guarantor, along with the League as moral guarantor. He was to successfully argue that the rehabilitation of the refugees as workers would produce a greater and richer Greece and thus guarantee the payment of the loan.[14] Finally, the acquisition of the loan was made possible by Greece's willingness to accept its onerous terms, which necessitated a very heavy burden of taxation, and to concede to the RSC extraordinary powers.

While most of the reasons for the delay in concluding the loan agreement were legitimate, others were simply mean spirited and the consequence of petty rivalries. Initially, despite Nansen's best efforts, the League, including its Secretary General, Sir Eric Drummond, had some reservations about the effectiveness of the plan for refugee settlement and its role in the enterprise. There was understandably the reluctance to get involved in a novel financial enterprise whose failure would severely undermine the prestige of the budding international organization. Also, for good reasons, action on the loan had to be delayed until the protracted negotiations for a peace treaty were concluded at Lausanne (July 24, 1923) and until the creation of the RSC two months later. Without a peace treaty, there was the widespread fear of renewed hostilities between Greece and Turkey over the issue of reparations and that Greece would use the loan for military purposes.[15] Without the creation of the RSC, the international

---

[12]*League of Nations*, Archives of Nansen's Office, C1320, Letter 216, June 28, 1923.
[13]Near East Relief, *Report to Congress for 1923*, New York 1924, p. 20.
[14]Vogt, *Fridtjof Nansen*, Chapter V.
[15]*LNOJ*, 5th Year, No. 10 (October 1924), p. 1300; and Gregorios Daphnis, *I Ellas metaxi*

money markets would be essentially closed to Greece. The loan agreement had to wait for the creation of the RSC, with the powers and staff needed to gain the confidence of the world's bankers.

Moreover, the decision for the loan was also held in abeyance until such time as the unconstitutional government of Greece was replaced by a constitutional one, fully recognized by the Powers; and there was a concern that the new government might not honor any deals made with the revolutionary regime of the colonels. The fear that a duly elected government would repudiate the loan agreements was voiced in the June 22, 1923, meeting of the Finance Committee. However, on the same day, in a confidential and apparently effective letter to members of the Finance Committee, Nansen argued that this fear was unfounded. The interests of Greece, he wrote, were based on its goodwill with the League for many years to come and that no Greek government would renounce the loan agreements. If it did so it would discredit itself.[16]

In any case, a constitutional regime was finally re-established in Greece following the December 16, 1923, elections, but it did little to reign in the contentious nature of Greek politics and to gain the confidence of the Financial Committee, whose support for the loan was closely connected with the achievement of internal political stability in Greece. The elections, in which the royalists abstained, brought to power Venizelos' Liberal Party (200 seats) and its Republican allies (120 seats), who were most outspoken in the denunciation of the Crown and in favor of a Republic. The refugee settlement program was neglected as disorders became widespread in Greece over this issue. When the new Greek parliament met in January 1924, Venizelos, the newly elected prime minister, weary of the strife, resigned and left Greece. Two months later, on March 25, the issue was decided in favor of a Republic, followed by a confirmatory plebiscite that returned two-thirds of the vote for the Republic.[17] Meanwhile, hav-

dio polemon, 1923–1940 [Greece between the two wars, 1923–1940], Vol. 1 (Athens, 1955), p. 268.

[16] League of Nations, Archives of Nansen's Office, C1320, June 28, 1923.

[17] With the exception of the Venizelos government of 1928–1932 and the Metaxas dicta-

ing run out of preliminary funding in the RSC, Morgenthau felt compelled to call a press conference, in which he informed the Greek public that unless there was political stability he would not be able to secure financial support for refugee settlement.[18] Not surprisingly, in April 1924, the Council of the League refused to approve an initial loan ". . . unless political developments in Greece in the immediate future are such as to offer a prospect of order and economic stability and the consequent improvement in the foreign credit of the country."[19] Similar warnings were issued by the Council for the second loan request in 1926 and 1927 when the Greeks asked for the balance of the £10 million.[20]

Finally, there was, for some time, outright opposition to the loan by France and the United States. In the case of France, it was the result of anti-Greek sentiments. This was best demonstrated by the response of M. Hanotaux, the French delegate in the Council, to the Greek delegate, Dimitrios Caclamanos, who had requested the support of the League for a Greek refugee loan in the spring of 1923. Hanotaux told him: "Address yourselves to bankers. We are not financiers here."[21] Moreover, not only did France decline to take part in the great humanitarian work of refugee settlement, it also held up the approval of the loan by the League until Greece made satisfactory arrangements to pay up its French war debt. [22]

---

torship of 1936–1940, there was little continuity or stability in Greek politics during the interwar years. Weak coalition or minority governments and the increasing involvement of the military in the political arena exposed the young Republic (1924–1936) to transitory dictatorships, *coups d'état*, corruption, and inefficiency.

[18]Morgenthau, *I Was Sent to Athens*, p. 112. Having run out of the initial loan of £1 million by Britain and stymied by the protracted negotiations for refugee loans, Morgenthau saw that the only solution for the RSC to continue its work was a second advance by the Bank of England. He went to London in the Spring of 1924 and used his influence to persuade Britain to lend the Bank of Greece another advance of £1 million, permitting the RSC to continue its work until the end of the year. *Ibid.*,175–205.

[19]*LNOJ* (April 1924), p. 510

[20]*Ibid.* (July 1926), (October 1926), (April 1927), and (September 1927). The Finance Committee of the League had sought to reduce the refugee loan to £6 million.

[21]D. Caclamanos, "Greece, Her Friends and Foes," *The Contemporary Review*, 159, No. 904 (April 1941): 369.

[22]Pentzopoulos, *The Balkan Exchange of Minorities and Its Impact upon Greece*, p. 82. Some of the reasons behind French anti-Greek sentiment include the pro-German policies of King Constantine during the great war, and the humiliation and heavy casualties suffered

In the case of the United States government, whose relief agencies had saved the lives of hundreds of thousands of Greek refugees, opposition to the loan was clearly not the result of anti-Greek sentiment.[23] It had to do with a long standing dispute between Washington and Athens over the Tripartite Loan of 1917–1918, through which the United States, along with Britain and France, sought to reinforce the finances of Greece, as it joined the Allies in the final stages of the war.[24] The United States had offered a credit line of $50 million, but paid only $15 million. Washington wanted Athens to give up its claim for the balance of the credit line and would not approve the refugee loan unless Greece withdrew its claim. In the end, the United States employed diplomatic coercion to induce Greece to renounce its claims to the 1918 credits in exchange for American permission to float a new foreign loan.[25]

In any case, by October 1924, conditions in Greece improved. With Morgenthau's strong support, the RSC received the first installment of the League sponsored refugee loan by the end of the year. Also, with the ratification of the Treaty of Lausanne by Greece, Turkey and

by France when in 1917 Royalist troops fired upon Allied detachments that had made their way to the Greek capital, following an ultimatum to the Greek government. French anti-Greek sentiment was primarily the result of France's pro-Kemalist policies and Franco-British rivalry in the Near East, in which Greece was seen as an instrument of British foreign policy.

[23]One of the most vociferous American opponents to U.S. participation in the RSC and the refugee loan was Colonel William Haskell, the American Red Cross Commissioner to Greece. He had a strong antipathy to the League, opposed the loan, and was negative on refugee settlement in Macedonia. He believed that the Greeks were lazy and corrupt and that the Powers must force Greece to seek solutions within the limits of its own resources. Cassimatis, *American Influence in Greece, 1917–1929*, p. 141; Clark, *Twice a Stranger*, p. 153; Pentzopoulos, *The Balkan Exchange of Minorities and its Impact upon Greece*, p. 75; and the letter of Haskell to the Chairman of the American Red Cross (Payne) of January 19, 1923, in *FRUS*, Vol. II, Washington 1938, p. 319. See also Marjorie Housepian, *The Smyrna Affair*, p. 203.

[24]On February 18, 1918, Britain, France, and the United States granted a three-part loan of $150 million to Greece. In return, Greece agreed to put nine divisions at the disposal of the Allies in the Balkan front. The United States had entered the war in April 1917 (but not against the Ottoman Empire), followed by Greece three months later. Its purpose was to make Greece a viable ally in the war against the Central Powers. The credits were needed by Greece for arms and military supplies.

[25]Cassimatis, *American Influence in Greece, 1917–1929*, pp. 142–143; and Clark, *Twice a Stranger*, pp. 151–152.

the Allied Powers in August 1923, it was now incumbent on the League to implement the population exchange agreement, and to set up the mixed commissions to carry out the liquidation of the properties left behind by the refugees and to prepare compensation payments for them. The exchange of some 400,000 Muslims for the 190,000 remaining Greeks scattered throughout Anatolia, primarily in the Pontos, Cappadocia, and Eastern Thrace, was completed by early 1925.[26] However, agreement could not be reached on compensation for the refugees.[27] Finally, in 1930, for reasons of national interest, Greece conceded to the Turkish proposition that the value of the properties of the 400,000 Muslim refugees was equal to the value of the properties left behind by the 1.3 million Greek refugees. In essence, the properties of the refugees were transferred, without compensation, to the Greek and Turkish governments, confirming a condition of long standing.[28]

### Beyond the Greek Refugee Crisis

With a functioning RSC assured, Nansen could now turn his attention to matters beyond the Greek refugee crisis. In the Assembly of the League, he became a vocal supporter of antislavery resolutions and played a major role in securing the adoption of a convention against forced labor in the colonial territories. Also, a fierce opponent of international aggression, Nansen assumed a leadership role in the preparation of the League's first disarmament conference and on issues of collective security.

---

[26]Some 1.1 million refugees had fled to Greece prior to the exchange agreement. The advantage of the agreement was that they too would be compensated for their abandoned properties.

[27]However, the nonexchangeable populations of Western Thrace and Constantinople could not be dealt with without serious difficulties. For the problems of the mixed commissions for the evaluation of properties and for who was exchangeable, see Psomiades, *The Eastern Question*, Chapter 8; also Commission Mixte pour l'Échange des Populations Grecques et Turques. *Acts, décisions, sentences arbitrales relatifs à l'échange des populations grecques et turques.* Vol. 1 (Istanbul, 1933).

[28]Commission Mixte pour l'Échange des Populations Grecques et Turques, pp.74–77.

Indeed, Nansen's first encounter with a clear act of international aggression came as early as the Corfu incident of 1923. On August 27, 1923, while an international commission was engaged in delimiting the frontiers between Greece and Albania, the chief of the mission, the Italian general Tellini, was murdered with four members of his staff by bandits, just inside Greek territory. The Greek government immediately began an investigation, but before it had time to report its findings, Italy presented an ultimatum, the terms of which were most humiliating and therefore unacceptable to Athens. Italy refused to grant any extension of time for the Greeks to complete their investigation. On August 31, 1923, an Italian fleet appeared before Corfu, bombarded the island, without warning, causing a number of casualties. Italian troops immediately occupied Corfu and its neighboring Greek islands. Mussolini explained that this was not an act of war but a temporary and peaceful measure, and the French under Poincaré supported him. The Greek government correctly appealed to the League, which was fortunately in session at that moment. The protests raised in the Assembly, led by Nansen and his Swedish and Danish colleagues, Branting and Zahle, were so vehement that Italy was finally obliged to give way, and Corfu was evacuated on September 27, 1923. Although not backed by their governments, Nansen, Branting, and Zahle even threatened to withdraw from Geneva if the League failed to intervene in the crisis. Italy accused "Nansen and other agents as provocateurs who [by their actions] hoped to send the British fleet to Corfu."[29] By taking strong action and by insisting that the Council of the League was competent to deal with this clear act of aggression, the representatives of the small powers at Geneva, led by Nansen, had saved the League from a complete disaster in its first encounter with international aggression. In the end, the Conference of Ambassadors that met in Paris and that had authorized General Tellini's mission, moved to prevent the incident from going to the Council of the League. Fearful of Italian repercussions if the case should be taken up by the League, they awarded an indemnity to Italy

---

[29]*DDI*, Salandra (Geneva) to Mussolini (Rome), September 7, 1923, pp. 201–202.

on the questionable grounds that there had been negligence on the part of the Greek authorities.[30]

From 1925 onwards, Nansen also devoted much of his time as the League's High Commissioner for Refugees to aiding Ottoman Armenian refugees. His experience with the Ottoman Greeks brought him in contact with their tragic fate.[31] Forgotten by the Allies and ignored by the Treaty of Lausanne, the Armenians opened up in Nansen an immense, untapped reservoir of sympathy. Thanks to his tireless efforts, thousands of Ottoman Armenian refugees, victims of the 1915 Turkish massacres, were resettled in the USSR in the Sovietized Republic of Armenia. In 1925 he toured Soviet Armenia with the goal of establishing there a "national home" for all Armenians, and in the following year, took on the project of settling some 40,000 unemployed Armenian refugees living in Syria, Lebanon, and Alexandretta. His request for funds for both projects met with little response. However, despite the lack of support and sufficient funding from the League and the Powers, Nansen worked unflaggingly for what appeared to be a lost cause. He did, however, manage to obtain a promise of £100,000 pounds from Armenian associations in America and Europe, and a lesser amount from the governments of Germany, Greece, Norway, Luxemburg, and Romania. With these funds, Nansen planned and carried out settlement works in Armenia, independently of the League.[32]

Nansen's last years helping the Armenians sapped much of his strength. Disappointed in his lack of progress and at the unwillingness of the international community to support the Armenian refugees, he returned to Norway in the winter of 1929. During a ski trip there, he was taken ill and three months later on May 13, 1930,

---

[30]For a detailed study of these events, see James Barros, *The Corfu Incident of 1923: Mussolini and the League of Nations* (Princeton: Princeton University Press, 1965); and the *LNOJ* for the year 1923.

[31]Together with the Greek refugees came 80,000 Armenians, which a poverty stricken Greece admitted with the same consideration as the Greek refugees, without distinction. Nansen was to help many of these Armenians to resettle in Soviet Armenia. I. K. Hassiotis, "Armenians," Richard Clogg, ed., *Minorities in Greece: Aspects of a Plural Society* (London: Hurst & Company, 1998), pp. 94–111.

[32]Clausen, *Dr. Fridtjof Nansen's Work*, pp. 11–13.

this fearless peacemaker and advocate of the weak and suffering died of a heart attack at home in his 69th year, at his beloved Polhøgda near Oslo. He was given a state funeral before cremation. However, according to his wishes, no eulogies adorn his simple grave stone in a quiet garden near his home. No dates are inscribed upon it—just the name: Fridtjof Nansen.[33]

[33]The League of Nations honored Nansen by creating in 1931 the Nansen Office for Refugees, which won the Nobel Peace Prize in 1938. In 1954, the League's successor, the United Nations, established the Nansen Medal, later named the Nansen Refugee Award, given annually to an individual organization "in recognition of extraordinary and dedicated service to refugees."

# Epilogue

This book has focused on a critical turn of events in the history of modern Greece, which culminated with the defeat of the Greek armed forces during the Asia Minor campaign of 1921–1922. It was followed by a compulsory and massive exchange of populations between Greece and Turkey. The reader has been exposed throughout these pages to the perennial dilemmas in international affairs between pragmatism and principle, and between power and justice.

From the time of Thucydides to the present, warfare has been a part of the human condition. As the realist saying goes, "the strong do what they can and the weak suffer what they must." And, over the centuries, innocent populations—especially those on the side of the vanquished—have suffered terrible consequences. As we have seen throughout the pages of this volume, the process of the fragmentation of the Ottoman Empire was accelerated during the Balkan Wars, World War I, and—finally—during Greece's disastrous Anatolian campaign. The "exchange" of populations after all these wars was formalized though postwar treaties and agreements that permitted the "voluntary" movement of ethnic/religious communities (mostly Moslem Turks being exchanged for Christian Bulgarians and Christian Greeks, respectively). Interestingly, however, after the Second Balkan War and World War I, Christian Bulgarians were also exchanged with Christian Greeks in western Thrace and eastern Macedonia.

A new element, without precedent in world affairs, was the *compulsory* exchange of populations, which was legitimized by the Treaty of Lausanne in 1923. This phenomenon has formed the heart, and hopefully the contribution, of this volume. The exchange raised serious questions about fundamental issues of human rights, such as freedom of choice and protection of life, liberty, and the pursuit of happiness. Using contemporary language, one could argue that the compulsory uprooting of over two million people became a form of internationally legitimized "ethnic cleansing." Debate among historians and political scientists will long continue as to the merits and demerits of this grand historical experiment, pitting ethnic homogeneity against sociocultural pluralism. Ultimately, however, the fact remains that, without the exchange, the Greek element—given subsequent demographic trends in Turkey and Greece—would have been considerably reduced as a percentage of Greece's total population.

A second major theme that has been running through the pages of this book is centered on the role of the individual (the role of statesmanship) in shaping the products of history. Two towering figures emerge as having deeply influenced the tide of events: Eleftherios Venizelos and Fridtjof Nansen. Venizelos, before the Anatolian disaster, had spearheaded the last phase of Greece's *Megali Idea.* Through prudent strategic alignments, which he secured during the Balkan Wars and in World War I, he more than doubled Greece's territory. However, following his unfortunate defeat in the 1920 national elections and the return of the Monarchists to power, the road to disaster became wide open. Venizelos, after the catastrophe, reoriented his priorities and entered a phase of damage control, state reconstruction/development, and political modernization in a hopefully stable and consolidated democratic society.

In all this, the giant figure of Fridtjof Nansen—a scholar, a writer, an explorer, a diplomat, and a humanist—was added as a virtual blessing, blending comfortably with the statesmanship of Eleftherios Venizelos. Nansen, as a functionary of his government, as an envoy to the League of Nations, as a philanthropist and consistent proponent of human rights, exemplified in prototype form the role of civil society in world politics. Through the actions of the League, with the constant presence of the International Red Cross, committed individuals such as Nansen sustained efforts to provide succor for the victims of the wars and to smooth the rough edges of previously unregulated acts of national governments. Ultimately, the painful choice of the compulsory uprooting of populations was viewed as a "lesser evil" by both Venizelos and Nansen. Subsequent historical developments have tended to vindicate their actions.

The trend toward ethnic disintegration continued after World War II, with the collapse of the British Empire and the rapid decololonization processes in the 1950s, the 1960s, and beyond. In the early 1990s, disaggregation of multiethnic states took a giant step following the breakup of the Soviet Union and the end of the Cold War. This centrifugal trend has been clearly exemplified by the remarkable rise in United Nations membership (51 at its birth in 1945, 193 members today). Paradoxically, however, the fragmentation trend is being challenged and reversed by a parallel and powerful, centripetal process of integration/unification, as exemplified by a steadily enlarging and deepening European Union. Multiethnic and multireligious (in one word, pluralist) entities are being formed gradually, sometimes painfully, in all five continents of our planet. But in a clear departure from past practices, the birth of these politically hybrid entities is not the result of the power of the sword but the power of persuasion, based on mutual interests. These and other regional integration experiments may, some time in the future, resolve the painful dilemma that has challenged nationalists and internationalists alike over the past two centuries.

# The Military Convention between the Allied Powers, the Government of the Grand National Assembly of Turkey and Greece
## October 11, 1922

CONVENTION MILITAIRE ENTRE LES PUISSANCES ALLIÉES,

LE GOUVERNEMENT DE LA GRANDE ASSEMBLÉE

NATIONALE DE TURQUIE et LA GRECE.

- ! - ! - ! - ! -

Conformement aux termes de la Note adressée au Gouvernement de la Grande Assemblée Nationale de Turquie par les Puissances Alliées le 23 Septembre 1922, et de la note adressée au Puissances Alliées par le Gouvernement de la Grande Assemblée Nationale de Turquie le 29 Septembre 1922, des réunions entre les Généraux Alliés :

   le Général HARINGTON, pour le Grande Bretagne,
   le Général LOMBELLI, pour l'Italie,
   le Général CHARPY, pour la France,
  et le Général ISMET PACHA, pour le Gouvernement de la
           Grande Assemblée Nationale de
           Turquie,
  et le Général MAZARAKIS, pour la Grèce,

ant été tenues à Moudania le 3 Octobre 1922 et jours suivants.

.
. .

Les Gouvernements alliés ayant décidé de remettre au Gouvernement de la Grande Assemblée Nationale de Turquie la Thrace Orientale y compris Andrinople, le but de cette conférence était :

1°. De préciser la ligne au delà de laquelle les forces grecques seront invitées à se retirer de la Thrace Orientale.

2°. d'établir les modalités d'évacuation des troupes et de l'administration helléniques et de l'installation de l'administration et de la gendarmerie du Gouvernement de la Grande Assemblée Nationale de Turquie dans ce territoire.

3°. d'assurer le contrôle de cette région pendant la période transitoire en vue de maintenir l'ordre et la sécurité publique.

.
. .

Les Délégués se sont mis d'accord sur les points suivants:

1°. Les hostilités cesseront entre les forces turques et helléniques à la date d'entrée en vigueur de la présente convention.

2°. La ligne derrière laquelle les troupes helléniques de Thrace seront invitées à se retirer dès la mise en vigueur de la présente convention est constituée par la rive gauche de la Maritza, de son embouchure dans la Mer Egée jusqu'au point où elle traverse la frontière de Thrace avec la Bulgarie.

3°. Afin d'éviter toutes complications possibles jusqu'à la conclusion de la paix, la rive droite de la Maritza (Kara Agatch inclus) sera occupée par des contingents alliés qui seront installés en des points à déterminer par les Alliés.

4°. La portion de voie ferrée longeant la rive droite de la Maritza de Swilengrad (Jisr Mustapha Pacha) à Kuléli-Bourgas sera l'objet d'une surveillance (à régler par une convention spéciale) par une Commission militaire mixte comprenant un Délégué de chacune des trois Puissances alliées, un Délégué de la Grande Assemblée Nationale de Turquie et un Délégué de la Grèce, en vue de maintenir intégralement le libre parcours de cette section de voie qui permet l'accès de la région d'Andrinople.

5°. L'évacuation de la Thrace Orientale par les troupes grecques commencera dès la mise en vigueur de cette convention. Elle comprendra les troupes elles-mêmes, les services et formations militaires et leurs moyens de transport divers, ainsi que les approvisionnements stockés en matériel de guerre, munitions, dépôts de vivres.

Cette évacuation sera effectuée dans le délai d'environ 15 jours.

6°. Les autorités civiles helléniques y compris la Gendarmerie, seront retirées aussitôt que possible. Au fur et à mesure que les Autorités helléniques se retireront de chaque région administrative, les pouvoirs civils seront remis aux autorités alliées qui les transmettront autant que possible le jour même aux autorités turques. Pour l'ensemble de la région de Thrace cette remise devra être terminée dans un délai maximum de 30 jours, après la fin de l'évacuation par les troupes grecques.

7°. Les fonctionnaires du Gouvernement de la Grande Assemblée Nationale de Turquie seront accompagnés de forces de gendarmerie du Gouvernement de la Grande Assemblée Nationale de Turquie, d'effectif strictement nécessaire au maintien de l'ordre et de la sécurité locale, à la surveillance de la frontière et des chemins de fer.

L'effectif total de ces forces ne dépassera pas : 8.000 (Officiers compris).

8°. Les opérations de retrait des troupes grecques et la transmission de l'administration civile s'effectueront sous la direction de missions interalliées qui seront installées dans les principaux centres. Le rôle de ces missions est de s'entremettre pour faciliter les opérations ci-dessus de retrait et de transmission. Elles s'efforceront d'empêcher les excès de toute nature.

9°. En outre de ces missions, des contingents alliés occuperont la Thrace Orientale.

10°. Le retrait des missions et des contingents alliés aura lieu 30 jours après que l'évacuation des troupes grecques aura été terminée.

Ce retrait pourra avoir lieu à une date plus rapprochée pourvu que les Gouvernements alliés soient d'accord pour considérer que des mesures suffisantes ont été prises pour le maintien de l'ordre et la protection des populations non turques. C'est ainsi que lorsque l'administration et la gendarmerie du Gouvernement de la Grande Assemblée nationale de Turquie fonctionneront régulièrement dans une division administrative, les missions et contingents alliés pourront être retirés de cette division administrative avant l'expiration du délai de 30 jours prévu.

11°. En Asie, les troupes du Gouvernement de la Grande Assemblée Nationale de Turquie s'arrêteront sur les lignes suivantes qui ne devront pas être dépassées jusqu'à l'ouverture et pendant la conférence de la paix : -

Région de Chanak :

Une ligne à une distance d'environ 15 kil. de la côte asiatique des Dardanelles ayant pour origine Koum Bournou au Sud et rejoignant Boz Bournou (Nord de Lampsaki) au Nord.

Péninsule d'Ismid :

Une ligne allant de Daridjé sur le Golfe d'Ismid, à Chilé sur la Mer Noire en passant par Guebzé. Ces localités incluses au Gouvernement de la Grande Assemblée Nationale de Turquie.

La route allant de Daridjé à Chilé pourra être utilisée en commun par les troupes alliées et celles du Gouvernement de la Grande Assemblée Nationale de Turquie.

Les lignes ci-dessus seront délimitées par des commissions mixtes composées d'un Officier de chacune des armées alliées et d'un Officier de l'armée du Gouvernement de la Grande Assemblée Nationale do Turquie.

Les Gouvernements alliés et le Gouvernement de la Grande Assemblée Nationale de Turquie, tout en prenant les précautions nécessaires pour prévenir tout incident, s'engagé à ne pas augmenter les effectifs de leurs troupes et à ne pas entreprendre de fortifications ou travaux militaires dans les régions ci-dessous :

Région de Chanak : à partir des Dardanelles jusqu'à une distance de 15 kil. à l'Est de la ligne Boz Bournou - Loum Bournou.

Péninsule d'Ismid : A partir du Bosphore jusqu'à une distance de 40 kil. à l'Est de la ligne Daridjé - Chilé.

Le Gouvernement de la Grande Assemblée Nationale de Turquie s'engage à ne pas placer d'Artillerie à moins de 15 kil. de la côte entre Boz Bournou (Nord de Lampsaki) et Kara Bournou (Nord de Kara Bigha) inclus.

12°. La présence des troupes alliées sera maintenue sur les territoires où elles sont stationnées actuellement, territoires que le Gouvernement de la Grande Assemblée Nationale de Turquie s'engage à respecter jusqu'à décision de la conférence de la paix :

Savoir :

Péninsule de Constantinople :

Toute la partie de la Péninsule située à l'Est de la ligne marquée par un point de la Mer Noire à 7 kil. nord Ouest de Podima, Istrandja, Kichtaghi, Sinekli, Kara-Sinan-Tchiflik, Kadi-Keuy, Yénidjé, Fladina-Tchiflik, Calicratia, tous ces points inclus.

Péninsule de Gallipoli :

Toute la partie de la Péninsule de Gallipoli au Sud de la ligne : Bakla - Bournou (Cap Xeros), Boulaïr, embouchure du Soghluck, tous ces points inclus.

13°. Le Gouvernement de la Grande Assemblée Nationale de Turquie s'engage à ne pas transporter de troupes ni à lever ou entretenir une armée en Thrace Orientale jusqu'à ratification du traité de paix.

14°. La présente convention entrera en vigueur 3 jours après sa signature, c'est-à-dire à minuit le 14/15 (quatorze/quinze) Octobre 1922. (N.S.)

Faite en quatre feuillets à LOUMANIA (en français),

ce onze Octobre , mil neuf cent vingt deux. (N.S.)


Pour la Grande Bretagne : -   *Th. Harington* L'Général

Pour l'Italie               : -

Pour la France              : -   *Ch. Charpy*

Pour le Gouvernement de
la Grande Assemblée         : -
Nationale de Turquie.

Pour la Grèce               : -

# The Convention Concerning the Exchange of Greek-Turkish Populations January 30, 1923[1]

The Government of the Grand National Assembly of Turkey and the Greek Government have agreed upon the following provisions:

### Article 1

As from the 1st May, 1923, there shall take place a compulsory exchange of Turkish nationals of the Greek Orthodox religion established in Turkish territory, and of Greek nationals of the Moslem religion established in Greek territory.

These persons shall not return to live in Turkey or Greece respectively without the authorisation of the Turkish Government or of the Greek Government respectively.

### Article 2

The following persons shall not be included in the exchange provided for in Article 1:

a) The Greek inhabitants of Constantinople.

b) The Moslem inhabitants of Western Thrace.

All Greeks who were already established before the October 30, 1918, within the areas under the Prefecture of the City of Constantinople, as defined by the law of 1912, shall be considered as Greek inhabitants of Constantinople.

All Moslems established in the region to the east of the frontier line laid

---

[1]Ratified by Turkey, August, 23, 1923, by Greece, August 25, 1923.

down in 1913 by the Treaty of Bucharest[2] shall be considered as Moslem inhabitants of Western Thrace.

### Article 3

Those Greeks and Moslems who have already, and since the October 18, 1912, left the territories the Greek and Turkish inhabitants of which are to be respectively exchanged, shall be considered as included in the exchange provided for in Article 1.

The expression "emigrant" in the present Convention includes all physical and juridical persons who have been obliged to emigrate or have emigrated since the October 18, 1912.

### Article 4

All able-bodied men belonging to the Greek population whose families have already left Turkish territory, and who are now detained in Turkey, shall constitute the first instalment of Greeks sent to Greece in accordance with the present Convention.

### Article 5

Subject to the provisions of Articles 9 and 10 of the present Convention, the rights of property and monetary assets of Greeks in Turkey or Moslems in Greece shall not be prejudiced in consequence of the exchange to be carried out under the present Convention.

### Article 6

No obstacle may be placed for any reason whatever in the way of the departure of a person belonging to the populations which are to be exchanged. In the event of an emigrant having received a definite sentence of imprisonment, or a sentence which is not yet definitive, or of his being the object of criminal proceedings, he shall be handed over by the authorities of the prosecuting country to the authorities of the country whither he is going, in order that he may serve his sentence or be brought to trial.

---

[2]British and Foreign State Papers, 107:658.

## Article 7

The emigrants will lose the nationality of the country which they are leaving, and will acquire the nationality of the country of their destination, upon their arrival in the territory of the latter country.

Such emigrants as have already left one or other of the two countries and have not yet acquired their new nationality shall acquire that nationality on the date of the signature of the present Convention.

## Article 8

Emigrants shall be free to take away with them or to arrange for the transport of their movable property of every kind, without being liable on this account to the payment of any export or import duty or any other tax.

Similarly, the members of each community (including the personnel of mosques, tekkes, medresses, churches, convents, schools, hospitals, socities, associations and juridical persons, or other foundations of any nature whatever) which is to leave the territory of one of the Contracting States under the present Convention, shall have the right to take away freely or to arrange for the transport of the movable property belonging to their communities.

The fullest facilities for transport shall be provided by the authorities of the two countries, upon the recommendation of the Mixed Commission provided for in Article 11.

Emigrants who may not be able to take away all or part of their movable property can leave it behind. In that event, the local authorities shall be required to draw up, the emigrant in question being given an opportunity to be heard, an inventory and valuation of the property left by him. Procés verbaux containing the inventory and valuation of the movable property left by the emigrant shall be drawn up in four copies, one of which shall be kept by the local authorities, the second transmitted to the Mixed Commission provided for in Article 11 to serve as the basis for the liquidation provided for by Article 9, the third shall be handed to the Government of the country to which the emigrant is going, and the fourth to the emigrant himself.

## Article 9

Immovable property, whether rural or urban, belonging to emigrants, or to the communities mentioned in Article 8, and the movable property left by these emigrants or communities, shall be liquidated in accordance with the following provisions by the Mixed Commission provided for in Article 13.

Property situated in the districts to which the compulsory exchange applies and belonging to religious or benevolent institutions of the communities established in a district to which the exchange does not apply, shall likewise be liquidated under the same conditions.

## Article 10

The movable and immovable property belonging to persons who have already left the territory of the High Contracting Parties and are considered, in accordance with Article 3 of the present Convention, as being included in the exchange of populations, shall be liquidated in accordance with Article 9. This liquidation shall take place independently of all measures of any kind whatever which, under the laws passed and the regulations of any kind made in Greece and in Turkey since the October 18, 1912, or in any other way, have resulted in any restriction on rights of ownership over the property in question, such as confiscation, forced sale, etc. In the event of the property mentioned in this article or in Article 9 having been submitted to a measure of this kind, its value shall be fixed by the Commission provided for in Article 11, as if the measures in question had not been applied.

As regards expropriated property, the Mixed Commission shall undertake a fresh valuation of such property, if it has been expropriated since October 18, 1912, having previously belonged to persons liable to the exchange of populations in the two countries, and is situated in territories to which the exchange applies. The Commission shall fix for the benefit of the owners such compensation as will repair the injury which the Commission has ascertained. The total amount of this compensation shall be carried to the credit of these owners and to the debit of the Government on whose territory the expropriated property is situated.

In the event of any persons mentioned in Articles 8 and 9 not having received the income from property, the enjoyment of which they have lost in one way or another, the restoration of the amount of this income shall be guaranteed to them on the basis of the average yield of the property before the war, and in accordance with the methods to be laid down by the Mixed Commission.

The Mixed Commission provided for in Article 11, when proceeding to the liquidation of Wakouf property in Greece and of the rights and interests connected therewith, and to the liquidation of similar foundations belonging to Greeks in Turkey, shall follow the principles laid down in previous Treaties with a view to fully safeguarding the rights and interests of these foundations and of the individuals interested in them.

The Mixed Commission provided for in Article 11 shall be entrusted with the duty of executing this provisions.

### Article 11

Within one month from the coming into force of the present Convention a Mixed Commission shall be set up in Turkey or in Greece consisting of four members representing each of High Contracting Parties, and of three members chosen by the Council of the League of Nations from among nationals of Powers which did not take part in the war of 1914-1918. The Presidency of the Commission shall be exercised in turn by each of three neutral members.

The Mixed Commission shall have the right to set up, in such places as it may appear to them necessary, Sub-Commissions working under its order. Each such Sub-Commission shall consist of a Turkish member, a Greek member and a neutral President to be designated by the Mixed Commission. The Mixed Commission shall decide the powers to be delegated to the Sub-Commission.

### Article 12

The duties of the Mixed Commission shall be to supervise and facilitate the emigration provided for in the present Convention, and to carry out the liquidation of the movable and immovable property for which provision is made in Articles 9 and 10.

The Commission shall settle the methods to be followed as regards the emigration and liquidation mentioned above.

In a general way the Mixed Commission shall have full power to take the measures necessitated by the execution of the present Convention and to decide all questions to which this Convention may give rise.

The decisions of the Mixed Commission shall be taken by a majority.

All disputes relating to property, rights and interests which are to be liquidated shall be settled definitely by the Commission.

## Article 13

The Mixed Commission shall have full power to cause the valuation to be made of the movable and immovable property which is to be liquidated under the present Convention, the interested parties being given a hearing or being duly summoned so that they may be heard.

The basis for valuation of the property to be liquidated shall be the value of the property in gold currency.

## Article 14

The Commission shall transmit to the owner concerned a declaration stating the sum due to him in respect of the property of which he has been dispossessed, and such property shall remain at the disposal of the Government on whose territory it is situated.

The total sums due on the basis of these declarations shall constitute a Government debt from the country where the liquidation takes place to the Government of the country to which the emigrant belongs. The emigrant shall in principle be entitled to receive in the country to which he emigrates, as representing the sums due to him, property of a value equal to and of the same nature as that which he has left behind.

Once every six months an account shall be drawn up of the sums due by the respective Governments on the basis of the declarations as above.

When the liquidation is completed, if the sums of money due to both sides correspond, the accounts relating thereto shall be balanced. If a sum remains due from one of the Governments to the other Government after a balance has been struck, the debit balance shall be paid in cash. If the debtor Government requests a postponement in making this payment, the Commission may grant such postponement, provided that the sum due be paid in three annuities at most. The Commission shall fix the interest to be paid during the period of postponement.

If the sum to be paid is fairly large and requires longer postponement, the debtor Government shall pay in cash a sum to be fixed by the Mixed Commission, up to a maximum of 20 percent of the total due and shall issue in respect of the balance loan certificates bearing such interest as the Mixed Commission may fix, to be paid off within 20 years at most. The debtor Government shall assign to the service of these loans pledges approved by the Commission, which shall be administered and of which the revenues shall be encashed by the International Commission in Greece and by the Council of the Public Debt at Constantinople. In the absence of agreement in regard to these pledges, they shall be selected by the Council of the League of Nations.

## Article 15

With a view to facilitating emigration, funds shall be advanced to the Mixed Commission by the States concerned, under conditions laid down by the said Commission.

## Article 16

The Turkish and Greek Governments shall come to an agreement with the Mixed Commission provided for in Article 11 in regard to all questions concerning the notification to be made to persons who are to leave the territory of Turkey and Greece under the present Convention, and concerning the ports to which these persons are to go for the purpose of being transported to the country of their destination.

The High Contracting Parties undertake mutually that no pressure direct or indirect shall be exercised on the populations which are to be exchanged with a view to making them leave their homes or abandon their property before the date fixed for their departure. They likewise undertake to impose on the emigrants who have left or who are to leave the country no special taxes or dues. No obstacle shall be placed in the way of the inhabitants of the districts excepted from the exchange under Article 2 exercising freely their right to remain in or return to those districts and to enjoy to the full their liberties and rights of property in Turkey and in Greece. This provision shall not be invoked as a motive for preventing the free alienation of property belonging to inhabitants of the said regions which are excepted from the exchange, or the voluntary departure of those among these inhabitants who wish to leave Turkey or Greece.

*Article 17*

The expenses entailed by the maintenance and working of the Mixed Commission and of the organisations dependent on it shall be borne by the Governments concerned in proportions to be fixed by the Commission.

*Article 18*

The High Contracting Parties undertake to introduce in their respective laws such modifications as may be necessary with a view to ensuring the execution of the present Convention.

# The Treaty of Lausanne,
# July 24, 1923

### *Article 1*

From the coming into force of the present Treaty, the state of peace will be definitely re-established between the British Empire, France-Italy, Japan, Greece, Roumania and the Serb-Croat-Slovene State of the one part, and Turkey of the other part, as well as between their respective nationals.

Official relations will be resumed on both sides and, in the respective territories, diplomatic and consular representatives will receive, without prejudice to such agreements as may be concluded in the future, treatment in accordance with the general principles of international law.

### *Article 2*

From the Black Sea to the Aegean the frontier of Turkey is laid down as follows.

(1) *With Bulgaria:*

From the mouth ol the River Rezvaya, to the River Maritza, the point of junction of the three frontiers of Turkey, Bulgaria and Greece:

the southern frontier of Bulgaria as at present demarcated;

(2) *With Greece:*

Thence to the confluence of the Arda and the Maritza:

the course of the Maritza;

then upstream along the Arda, up to a point on that river to be determined on the spot in the immediate neighbourhood of the village of Tchörek-Keuy:

the course of the Arda;

thence in a south-easterly direction up to a point on the Maritza, 1 kilom. below Bosna-Keuy:

a roughly straight line leaving in Turkish territory the village of Bosna-Keuy. The village of Tchörek-Keuy shall be assigned to Greece or to Turkey according as the majority of the population shall be found to be Greek or Turkish by the Commission for which provision is made in Article 5, the population which has migrated into this village after the 11th October, 1922, not being taken into account;

thence to the Aegean Sea:

the course of the Maritza. . . .

### Article 12

The decision taken on the 13th February, 1914, by the Conference of London, in virtue of Articles 5 of the Treaty([2]) of London of the 17th-30th May, 1913, and 15 of the Treaty([3]) of Athens of the 1st-14th Novernber, 1913, which decision was communicated to the Greek Government on the 13th February, 1914, regarding the sovereignty of Greece over the islands of the Eastern Mediterranean, other than the islands of Imbros, Tenedos and Rabbit Islands, particularly the islands of Lemnos, Samothrace, Mytilene, Chios, Samos and Nikaria, is confirmed, subject to the provisions of the present Treaty respecting the islands placed under the sovereignty of Italy which form the subject of Article 15.

Except where a provision to the contrary is contained in the present Treaty, the islands situated at less than three miles from the Asiatic coast remain under Turkish sovereignty.

### Article 13

With a view to ensuring the maintenance of peace, the Greek Government undertakes to observe the following restrictions in the islands of Mytilene, Chios, Samos and Nikaria:

1. No naval base and no fortification will be established in the said islands.

2. Greek military aircraft will be forbidden to fly over the territory of the Anatolian coast. Reciprocally, the Turkish Government will forbid their military aircraft to fly over the said islands.

3. The Greek military forces in the said islands will be limited to the normal contingent called up for military service, which can be trained on the spot, as well as to a force of gendarmerie and police in proportion to the force of gendarmerie and police existing in the whole of the Greek territory.

## Article 14

The islands of Imbros and Tenedos, remaining under Turkish sovereignty, shall enjoy a special administrative organisation composed of local elements and furnishing every guarantee for the native non-Moslem population in so far as concerns local administration and the protection of person and property. The maintenance of order will be assured therein by a police force recruited from amongst the local population by the local administration above provided for and placed under its orders. The agreements which have been, or may be, concluded between Greece and Turkey relating to the exchange of the Greek and Turkish populations will not be applied to the inhabitants of the islands of Imbros and Tenedos.

## Article 15

Turkey renounces in favour of Italy all rights and title over the following islands: Stampalia (Astrapalia), Rhodes (Rhodos), Calki (Kharki), Scarpanto, Casos (Casso), Piscopis (Tilos), Misiros (Nisyros), Calimnos (Kalymnos), Leros, Patmos, Lipsos (Lipso), Simi (Symi), and Cos (Kos), which are now occupied by Italy, and the islets dependent thereon, and also over the island of Castellorizo.

## Article 16

Turkey hereby renounces all rights and title whatsoever over or respecting the territories situated outside the frontiers laid down in the present Treaty and the islands other than those over which her sovereignty is recognised by the said Treaty, the future of these territories and islands being settled or to be settled by the parties concerned. The provisions of the present Article do not prejudice any special arrangements arising from neighbourly relations which have been or may be concluded between Turkey and any limitrophe countries. . . .

## Article 20

Turkey hereby recognises the annexation of Cyprus proclaimed by the British Government on the 5th November, 1914.

*Article 21*

Turkish nationals ordinarily resident in Cyprus on the 5th November, 1914, will acquire British nationality subject to the conditions laid down in the local law, and will thereupon lose their Turkish nationality. They will, however, have the right to opt for Turkish nationality within two years from the coming into force of the present Treaty, provided that they leave Cyprus within twelve months after having so opted.

Turkish nationals ordinarily resident in Cyprus on the coming into force of the present Treaty who, at that date, have acquired or are in process of acquiring British nationality, in consequence of a request made in accordance with the local law, will also thereupon lose their Turkish nationality.

It is understood that the Government of Cyprus will be entitled to refuse British nationality to inhabitants of the island who, being Turkish nationals, had formerly acquired another nationality without the consent of the Turkish Government. . . .

*Article 37*

Turkey undertakes that the stipulations contained in Articles 38 to 44 shall be recognised as fundamental laws, and that no law, no regulation, nor official action shall conflict or interfere with these stipulations, nor shall any law, regulation, nor official action prevail over them.

*Article 38*

The Turkish Government undertakes to assure full and complete protection of life and liberty to all inhabitants of Turkey without distinction of birth, nationality, language, race or religion.

All inhabitants of Turkey shall be entitled to free exercise, whether in public or private, of any creed, religion or belief, the observance of which shall not be incompatible with public order and good morals.

Non-Moslem minorities will enjoy full freedom of movement and of emigration, subject to the measures applied, on the whole or on part of the territory, to all Turkish nationals, and which may be taken by the Turkish Government for national defence, or for the maintenance of public order.

## Article 39

Turkish nationals belonging to non-Moslem minorities will enjoy the same civil and political rights as Moslems.

All the inhabitants of Turkey, without distinction of religion, shall be equal before the law.

Differences of religion, creed or confession shall not prejudice any Turkish national in matters relating to the enjoyment of civil or political rights, as, for instance, admission to public employments, functions and honours, or the exercise of professions and industries. No restrictions shall be imposed on the free use by any Turkish national of any language in private intercourse, in commerce, religion, in the press, or in publications of any kind or at public meetings. Notwithstanding the existence of the official language, adequate facilities shall be given to Turkish nationals of non-Turkish speech for the oral use of their own language before the Courts.

## Article 40

Turkish nationals belonging to non-Moslem minorities shall enjoy the same treatment and security in law and in fact as other Turkish nationals. In particular, they shall have an equal right to establish, manage and control at their own expense, any charitable, religious and social institutions, any schools and other establishments for instruction and education, with the right to use their own language and to exercise their own religion freely therein.

## Article 41

As regards public instruction, the Turkish Government will grant in those towns and districts, where a considerable proportion of non-Moslem nationals are resident, adequate facilities for ensuring that in the primary schools the instruction shall be given to the children of such Turkish nationals through the medium of their own language. This provision will not prevent the Turkish Government from making the teaching of the Turkish language obligatory in the said schools. In towns and districts where there is a considerable proportion of Turkish nationals belonging to non-Moslem minorities, these minorities shall be assured an equitable share in the enjoyment and application of the sums which may be provided out of public funds under the State, municipal or other budgets for educational, religious, or charitable purposes.

The sums in question shall be paid to the qualified representatives of the establishments and institutions concerned.

### Article 42

The Turkish Government undertakes to take, as regards non-Moslem minorities, in so far as concerns their family law or personal status, measures permitting the settlement of these questions in accordance with the customs of those minorities.

These measures will be elaborated by special Commissions composed of representatives of the Turkish Government and of representatives of each of the minorities concerned in equal number. In case of divergence, the Turkish Government and the Council of the League of Nations will appoint in agreement an umpire chosen from amongst European lawyers.

The Turkish Government undertakes to grant full protection to the churches, synagogues, cemeteries, and other religious establishments of the above-mentioned minorities. All facilities and authorisation will be granted to the pious foundations, and to the religious and charitable institutions of the said minorities at present existing in Turkey, and the Turkish Government will not refuse, for the formation of new religious and charitable institutions, any of the necessary facilities which are granted to other private institutions of that nature.

### Article 43

Turkish nationals belonging to non-Moslem minorities shall not be compelled to perform any act which constitutes a violation of their faith or religious observances, and shall not be placed under any disability by reason of their refusal to attend Courts of Law or to perform any legal business on their weekly day of rest.

This provision, however, shall not exempt such Turkish nationals from such obligations as shall be imposed upon all other Turkish nationals for the preservation of public order.

### Article 44

Turkey agrees that, in so far as the preceding Articles of this Section affect non-Moslem nationals of Turkey, these provisions constitute obligations of international concern and shall be placed under the guarantee of the League of Nations. They shall not be modified without the assent of the majority of the Council of the League of Nations. The British Empire, France, Italy and Japan hereby agree not to withhold their assent to any modification in these Articles which is in due form assented to by a majority of the Council of the League of Nations.

Turkey agrees that any Member of the Council of the League of Nations shall have the right to bring to the attention of the Council any infraction or danger of infraction of any of these obligations, and that the Council may thereupon take such action and give such directions as it may deem proper and effective in the circumstances.

Turkey further agrees that any difference of opinion as to questions of law or of fact arising out of these Articles between the Turkish Government and any one of the other Signatory Powers or any other Power, a member of the Council of the League of Nations, shall be held to be a dispute of an international character under Article 14 of the Covenant of the League of Nations. The Turkish Government hereby consents that any such dispute shall, if the other party thereto demands, be referred to the Permanent Court of International Justice. The decision of the Permanent Court shall be final and shall have the same force and effect as an award under Article 13 of the Covenant.

## Article 45

The rights conferred by the provisions of the present Section on the non-Moslem minorities of Turkey will be similarly conferred by Greece on the Moslem minority in her territory. . . .

## Article 59

Greece recognises her obligation to make reparation for the damage caused in Anatolia by the acts of the Greek army or administration which were contrary to the laws of war.

On the other hand, Turkey, in consideration of the financial situation of Greece resulting from the prolongation of the war and from its consequences, finally renounces all claims for reparation against the Greek Government. . . .

*Article 106*

When, as a result of the fixing of new frontiers, a railway connection between two parts of the same country crosses another country, or a branch line from one country has its terminus in another, the conditions of working, in so far as concerns the traffic between the two countries, shall, subject to any special arrangements, be laid down in an agreement to be concluded between the railway administrations concerned. If these administrations cannot come to an agreement as to the terms of such agreement, those conditions shall be decided by arbitration.

The establishment of all new frontier stations between Turkey and the neighbouring States, as well as the working of the lines between those stations, shall be settled by agreements similarly concluded.

*Article 107*

Travellers and goods coming from or destined for Turkey or Greece, and making use in transit of the three sections of the Oriental Railways included between the Greco-Bulgarian frontier and the Greco-Turkish frontier near Kuleli-Burgas, shall not be subject, on account of such transit, to any duty or toll nor to any formality of examination in connection with passports or customs.

A Commissioner, who shall be selected by the Council of the League of Nations, shall ensure that the stipulations of this Article are carried out.

The Greek and Turkish Governments shall each have the right to appoint a representative to be attached to this Commissioner; this representative shall have the duty of drawing the attention of the Commissioner to any question relating to the execution of the above-mentioned stipulations, and shall enjoy all the necessary facilities to enable him to accomplish his task. These representatives shall reach an agreement with the Commissioner as to the number and nature of the subordinate staff which they will require.

It shall be the duty of the said Commissioner to submit, for the decision of the Council of the League of Nations, any question relating to the execution of the said stipulations which he may not have been able to settle. The Greek and Turkish Governments undertake to carry out any decision given by the majority vote of the said Council.

The salary of the said Commissioner, as well as the expenses of his work, shall be borne in equal parts by the Greek and Turkish Governments.

In the event of Turkey constructing later a railway line joining Adrianople to the line between Kuleli-Burgas and Constantinople, the stipulations of this Article shall lapse in so far as concerns transit between the points on the Greco-Turkish frontier lying near Kuleli-Burgas and Bosna-Keuy respectively.

Each of the two interested Powers shall have the right, after five years from the coming into force of the present Treaty, to apply to the Council of the League of Nations with a view to deciding whether it is necessary that the control mentioned in paragraphs 2 to 5 of the present Article should be maintained. Nevertheless, it remains understood that the stipulations of paragraph 1 shall remain in force for transit over the two sections of the Oriental Railways between the Greco-Bulgarian frontier and Bosna-Keuy.

### Article 142

The separate Convention concluded on the 30th January, 1923, between Greece and Turkey, relating to the exchange of the Greek and Turkish populations, will have as between these two High Contracting Parties the same force and effect as if it formed part of the present Treaty.

# Works Consulted

*Archival Collections*

France

Ministère des Relations Extérieures, Paris. Series "E", 1918–1929. Levant, Turquie.

Great Britain

National Archives (formerly the Public Record Office—PRO), Foreign Office Archives, Kew, London: FO 371 (General Correspondence).

Greece

The Diplomatic and Historical Archives of the Ministry of Foreign Affairs, 1914–1924, Athens.
Papers of Eleftherios Venizelos (1864–1936), Benaki Museum, Historical Archives, Penelope Delta House, Kifisia.
Papers of Alexander Mazarakis-Ainian (1874–1943), the National Historical and Ethnological Foundation of Greece, Athens.

League of Nations

Papers of Fridtjof Nansen (1861–1930), League of Nations Archives, the United Nations Library, Geneva.
League of Nations Archives, General Collection, 1920–1930, Geneva.

The United States

Papers of Mark A. Bristol (1868–1939) and Papers of Henry Morgenthau, Sr. (1856–1946), National Archives, Library of Congress, Manuscript Division, Washington, D.C.

*Published Official Documents*

France

Ministère des Affaires Étrangères, *Documents Diplomatiques,* "Conference de Lausanne," Vol. 1. Paris 1923.
———, Recueil (1). *Conférence de Lausanne sur lesaffaires du Proche-Orient (1922–1923). Recueil des acts de la Conference,* Première Série, Vols. I, II, III, IV, Paris 1925.

_____, Recueil (2). *Ibid.*, Deuxième Série, Vols. I, II, Paris 1923.

Great Britain

Foreign Office, *Documents on British Foreign Policy, 1919–1939*, First Series, Vols. I- XVIII. London 1947–1972. Especially Vol. XVII: Greece and Turkey, January 1, 1921-September 2, 1922 (1970) and Vol. XVIII: Greece and Turkey, September 3, 1922-July 24, 1923 (1972).

Foreign Office, *British and Foreign State Papers. 1923*, "Protocol Relating to the Settlement of Refugees in Greece and the Creation for this Purpose of a Refugee Settlement Commission, September 29, 1923,"(Geneva). Part II, Vol. CXVIII, London 1926, pp. 906–909; and "Annex Organic Statutes of the Greek Settlement Commission," pp. 909–912.

Foreign Office, *Miscellaneous No. 3 (1922).* "Pronouncement of the Three Allied Ministers of Foreign Affairs representing the Near East Situation, March 27, 1922 (Paris)," Cmd. 1641, London 1922.

*Parliamentary Papers, 1923. Turkey*, No. 1. Cmd. 1814. "Lausanne Conference on Near Eastern Affairs, 1922–1923." (Proceedings), London 1923.

Historical Archives, No. 8, *Turkey*, [E 1431/4/44], "Report on Refugees in the Near East by Dr. Nansen, High Commissioner of the League of Nations," January 26, 1923.

*Treaty Series* (1920), "Tripartite Agreement between the British Empire, France and Italy respecting Anatolia. . . ." Cmd. 963, London 1920; Treaty of Sèvres, August 19, 1920. Cmd 564, London 1920, and Treaty of Neuilly, November 27, 1919. Cmd. 522, London 1920.

Greece

Ministry of Foreign Affairs, *Greek Diplomatic Documents, 1919–1940*, Vol. III, *Greece and Turkey*, "Conference of Lausanne, 20 November 1922–24 July 1923," Athens 1994.

_____, *Diplomatic Documents, 1913–1917*, "The Greek White Book," New York 1919.

Ministère des Affaires Étrangères, *Les Persécutions anti-grecques en turquie de 1908 à 1921*, Athens 1921.

Vouliton Ellinon [Parliament of Greece], *Efimeris ton sizitiseon tis Voulis* [Journal of Debates of Parliament], Athens 1923–1930.

Italy

Ministero degli Affari Esteri. *I Documenti Diplomatici Italiani*. Series 6: November 5, 1918–October 30, 1922; and Series 7: October 31, 1922–April 14, 1935. Rome 1953,1955.

League of Nations

*Official Journal,* Geneva, 1920–1933.
*Treaty Series,* Geneva, 1920–1933.
*The Settlement of the Greek Refugees, Scheme for an International Loan, October 30, 1924,* Geneva 1924.
*Greek Stabilization and Refugee Loan—Protocol and Annexes, November 14, 1927,* Geneva 1927.
*The Question of the Exchange of Populations between Greece and Turkey, November 15, 1922,* Geneva 1922.
*L'établissement des réfugiés en Grèce,* Geneva 1926.


Turkey

*Büyük Millet Meclisizabitceridesi [Records of the Grand National Assembly],* Vol. 2, Ankara 1931.
*Lozan Telegraflari,* Ankara 1954.


United States

Department of State, *Foreign Relations of the United States,1923,* Vol. 2. Washington, D.C. 1938.
———. *Foreign Relations of the United States,1919,* "The Paris Peace Conference, 1919." Vol 3. Washington, D.C. 1943.
The U.S. House of Representatives. *Reports of the Near East Relief for the Years Ending December 31, 1922, December 31, 1923 and December 31, 1924. Washington, D.C., 1922,1923, 1924* respectively.
*Annual Report of the American Red Cross for the Year ending June 30, 1923,* Washington, D.C. 1923.


Commission Mixte pour l'Échange des Populations Grecques et Turques

*Actes, décisions, sentences arbitrales relatifs à l'échanges des populations grecques et turques.* Vol. 1, Istanbul 1933.
Martens, *Nouveau recueil général de traités.* Series 3, Leipzig 1876–1923.


*Diaries and Memoirs*

Alexandris, Apostolos, *Politikes anamniseis* [Political recollections] (Patras, 1947).
Aralov, S.I., *Vospominaniya Sovietskovo Diplomata, 1922–1923* [Memoirs of a Soviet diplomat, 1922–1923] (Moscow, 1960).
———, "In the Turkey of Atatürk," *International Affairs* [Moscow] 8 (August 1960): 81–87.
Argyropoulos, Pericles A., *Apomnimonevmata* [Memoirs] (Athens 1970).
Bierstadt, Edward Hale, *The Great Betrayal* (New York: R.M. McBride, 1924).

Caclamanos, D., "Greece, her Friends and Foes," *The Contemporary Review* 159, no. 904 (April 1944): 369–379.

Cebesoy, Ali Fuad, *Siyasî hatîralarî* [Political memoirs] (Istanbul 1957).

———, *Milli mücadele hatîralarî* [Recollections of the national struggle], Vol. I. (Istanbul, 1953).

Child, Richard W., *A Diplomat Looks at Europe* (New York, 1925).

Churchill, Winston, *The World Crisis: The Aftermath, 1918–1928,* Vol. V (New York: T. Butterworth, 1929).

Djemal, Pasha, *Memories of a Turkish Statesman, 1913–1919* (London: Hutchinson, 1924).

Eddy, Charles B., *Greece and the Greek Refugees* (London: G. Allen & Unwin, 1931).

Gonatas, Stylianos, *Apomnimonevmata, 1897–1957* [Memoirs, 1897–1957] (Athens, 1958).

Grew, Joseph G., *Turbulent Era: A Diplomatic Record of Forty Years, 1904–1945,* Vol. I (Boston: Houghton Mifflin, 1952).

Hardinge, Lord, *Old Diplomacy* (London: Murray, 1947).

Harington, Sir Charles, *Tim Harington Looks Back* (London: Murray, 1941).

Henderson, Sir Neville, *Water under the Bridges* (London: Hodder & Stoughton, 1945).

Horton, George, *The Blight of Asia* (New York: Bobbs Merrill, 1926).

———, *Report on Turkey: USA Consular Documents* (Athens, 1985).

Howland, Charles, "Greece and Her Refugees," *Foreign Affairs* 4 (July 1926): 613–623.

Inönü, Ismet, "Negotiations and the National Interest," *Perspectives on Peace, 1910–1960,* ed, Carnegie Endowment for International Peace (New York, 1960), pp. 135–150.

Jacquith, H.C., "America's Aid to 1,000,000 Near East Refugees," *Current History* 21, no. 3 (December 1924).

Karacan, Ali Naci, *Lozan konferansi ve Ismet Pasa* (Istanbul, 1943).

Kemal, Mustapha (Atatürk), *A Speech Delivered by Ghazi Mustapha Kemal, October 1927* (Leipzig: K. F. Koehler, 1929).

Kerr, Stanley E., *The Lions of Marash: Personal Experiences with American Near East Relief, 1919–1922* (Albany: State University of New York Press, 1973).

Laroche, Jules, *Au Quai d'Orsay avec Briand et Poincaré, 1913–1925* (Paris: Hachette, 1957).

Lloyd George, David, *The Truth About the Peace Treaties,* Vol.2 (London: V. Gollancz Ltd., 1938).

Mackenzie, Compton, *Greek Memories* (London: Cassell and Company Ltd., 1932).

Mazarakis-Ainian, Alexander, *Memoires* (Thessaloniki, 1979).

Morgenthau, Henry, *I Was Sent to Athens* (New York: Doubleday, Doran & Company, 1929).

Nansen, F., "Re-Making Greece." *Forum* (January 1924): 18–25.

_____, "Refugees and the Exchange of Populations," *The Encyclopedia Britannica*, 14th printing, Vol. 19 (London, 1929).

Nansen, Fridtjof, *Armenia and the Near East* (London: G. Allen & Unwin, 1928).

_____, *Farthest North*, Vol. II (London: G. Newnes, 1897).

Nicolopoulos, John, "The Testimony of Michail Vassilievich Frunze Concerning the Tragedy of Pontic Hellenism," *Journal of Modern Hellenism*, no. 4 (1987): 37–53.

Noel-Baker, Francis, *Greece, the Whole Story* (London: Hutchinson, 1946).

Nour, Riza, *Hayat ve Hatiratim* [My life and memories] (Istanbul: Garanti Matbaasi, 1967).

Pangalos, Theodoros, *Apomnimonevmata* Memoirs, 2 vols. (Athens, 1950, 1959).

Paraskevopoulos, L.I., *Anamnisis* [Memoirs] (Athens, 1933).

Rapp, W.J., *The Second Annual Report of the Athens American Relief Committee on Refugee Conditions in Greece and the Greek Islands, 1923* (Athens, 1923).

Rawlinson, Colonel Toby, *Adventures in the Near East, 1918–1922* (London: Melrose, 1923).

Riddel, Lord, *Intimate Diary of the Peace Conference and After* (London: Gollancz, 1933).

Simpson, Sir John Hope, *The Refugee Problem* (London: Oxford University Press, 1939).

Söylemezoğlu, Calib Kemali, *Hatılarlar* [Memoirs] (Istanbul, 1946).

Theotokas, Mihali, *O Eleftherios Venizelos eis tin syndiaskepsion tis Lozannis,1922–1923* [Eleftherios Venizelos at the Lausanne Conference, 1922–1923] (Athens, 1931).

Ward, Mark H., The Deportations of Asia Minor, 1921–1922 (London: Anglo-Hellenic League & British Armenia Committee, 1922).

## Biography

Alastos, Doros, *Venizelos* (London: Lund, 1942.)

Armstrong, H.C., *Grey Wolf: Mustafa Kemal; an Intimate Study of a Dictator*, (New York: Methuen, 1961).

Clausen, Clarence A., *Dr. Fridtjof Nansen's Work as High Commissioner of the League of Nations* (Urbana: University of Illinois, 1932) [thesis abstract].

Greve, T., *Fridtjof Nansen*, 2 vols. (Oslo: Gyldendal, 1974).

Hatziantoniou, Kostas, *Nicholas Plastiras* (Athens, 2006).

Høyer, Liv Nansen, *Nansen: A Family Portrait*. Translated from the Norwegian by Maurice Michael (London: Longmans, Green, 1957).

Huntford, Ronald, *Nansen: The Explorer as Hero* (London: Abacus, 1997).

Innes, Kathleen E., *The Story of Nansen and the League of Nations* (London: Friends Peace Committee, 1931).

Kinross, Lord, *Atatürk*, (London: Weidenfeld and Nicolson, 1996).

Kitromilides, Paschalis M., ed., *Eleftherios Venizelos: Trials of Statesmanship* (Edinburgh: Edinburgh University Press, 2006).

Nicolson, Harold, *Curzon: The Last Phase, 1919–1925; a Study in Post-war Diplomacy* (London: Constable, 1937).

_____, *Peacemaking 1919* (London: Houghton Mifflin, 1933).

Peponis, I.A., *Nicholas Plastiras, 1909–1945.* Vol.I (Athens, 1947).

Reynolds, E.E., *Nansen* (Harmondsworth: Penguin, 1949).

Ronaldshay, Earl of, *The Life of Lord Curzon.* Vol. 3 (London: Boni and Liveright, 1929).

Roskill, Stephen W., *Hankey: Man of Secrets.* Vol. II, 1919–1931 (London: Collins, 1972).

Ryne, Linn, *Fridtjof Nansen: Man of Many Facets* (Oslo 2010) net/norway/nansen.htm

Shackleton, Edward, *Nansen, the Explorer* (London: H.F. & G. Witherby, 1959).

Sørensen, Jon, *The Saga of Fridtjof Nansen.* Translated from the Norwegian by J.B.C. Watkins (New York: Norton, 1932).

Stefanos, Stefanos I., *Eleftherios Venizelos* (Athens, 1979).

Sveen, Asie, *Fridtjof Nansen: Scientist and Humanitarian,* March 15, 2001 in Nobelprize.org

Vogt, Per, *Fridtjof Nansen* (Oslo: Dreyer Forlag, 1961).

*General Works*

Akçam, Taner, *A Shameful Act: The Armenian Genocide and the Question of Turkish Responsibility* (New York: Metropolitan, 2006).

Barros, James, *The Corfu Incident of 1923: Mussolini and the League of Nations* (Princeton: Princeton University Press, 1965).

Barton, James L., *The Story of Near East Relief, 1915–1930: An Interpretation* (New York: Macmillan, 1930).

Bayur, Yusuf Hikmet, *Türk Inkilâbı Tarihi* [History of the Turkish reform], 2:3 (Ankara: Türk Tarih Kurumu Basimevi, 1951).

Bell-Fialkoff, Andrew, *Ethnic Cleansing* (New York: St. Martin's, 1996).

Bierstadt, Edward Hale, *The Great Betrayal* (New York: R.M. McBride, 1924).

Bıyıklıoğlu, Tevfik, *Trakya'da milli mücadele* [The struggle in Thrace], Vol. 2 (Ankara: Türk Tarih Kurumu Basimevi, 1956).

Bonsal, S., *Suitors and Suppliants: The Little Nations at Versailles* (New York: Prentice-Hall, 1946).

Busch, Briton Cooper, *Mudros to Lausanne: Britain's Frontier in West Asia, 1918–1923,* (Albany: State University of New York Press, 1976).

Cassimatis, Louis P., *The American Influence in Greece, 1917–1929* (Kent, OH: Kent State University Press, 1988).

Chrysanthos, Archbishop, *I ekklesia Trapezountos [The Church of Trebizond]* (Athens: Epitrope Pontiakon Meleton, 1973).

Clark, Bruce, *Twice a Stranger: The Mass Expulsions that Forged Modern Greece and Turkey* (London: Granta Books, 2006).

Cumming, Henry H., *Franco-British Rivalry in the Post-War Near East: The Decline of French Influence* (London: Oxford University Press, 1938).

Dakin, Douglas, *The Unification of Greece, 1770–1923* (London: E. Benn, 1972).

Daniel, Robert L., *American Philanthropy and the Near East, 1820–1960* (Athens, Ohio: Ohio University Press, 1970).

Daphnis, Georgos, *I Ellas metaxi dio polemon, 1923–1940* [Greece between the two wars, 1923–1940], Vol. 2 (Athens, 1955).

Devedji, Alexandre, *L'échange obligatoire des minorités grecques et turques en vertu de la convention de Lausanne du 30 Janvier 1923* (Paris: P. Bossuet, 1929).

Frangulis, A.F., *La Grèce et la Crise Mondiale,* Vol. 2 (Paris: F. Alcan, 1926).

Giannakopoulos, Georgos A., ed., *Refugee Greece* (Athens, 1992).

Giannuli, Dimitra M., *American Philanthropy in the Near East: Relief to the Ottoman Greek Refugees, 1922–1923* (Ph.D. Dissertation, Kent State University, 1992).

Hepburn, A.C., ed., *Minorities in History* (London: St. Martin's Press, 1978).

Hirschon, Renée, ed., *Crossing the Aegean: An Appraisal of the 1923 Compulsory Population Exchange* (Oxford: Berghahn Books, 2003).

Horton, George, *The Blight of Asia* (New York: Bobbs Merrill, 1926).

Housepian, Marjorie, *The Smyrna Affair* (New York: Harcourt Brace Jovanovich, 1966).

Howard, Harry N., *The Partition of Turkey. A Diplomatic History, 1913–1923* (Norman: University of Oklahoma Press, 1931).

Kiosseoglou, Th. P., *L'échange forcé des minorités d'après le traité de Lausanne* (Nancy: Imprimerie Nancéienne, 1926).

Ladas, Stephen P., *The Exchange of Minorities: Bulgaria, Greece and Turkey* (New York: Macmillan, 1932).

Macartney, C.A., *Refugees—The Work of the League* (London: League of Nations Union, 1931).

Macmillan, Margaret, *Paris 1919: Six Months that Changed the World* (New York: Random House, 2002).

Marrus, M., *The Unwanted European Refugees in the Twentieth Century* (Oxford: Oxford University Press, 1985).

Mavrocordatos, George T., *Stillborn Republic: Social Coalitions and Party Strategies in Greece, 1922–1936* (Berkeley: University of California Press, 1982).

Mears, Eliot G., *Modern Turkey* (New York: Macmillan, 1924).

Milton, Giles, *Paradise Lost, Smyrna 1922, the Destruction of Islam's City of Tolerance* (London: Sceptre, 2008).

Oran, Baskin, *Türk-Yunan İlişkilerinde Batı Trakya Sorunu* [Turkish-Greek relations and the Question of Western Thrace], 2nd Edition (Ankara: Bilgi Yayinevi, 1991).

Pagtziloglu, Milton, *I genoktonia ton Ellinon kai ton Armenion tis Mikras Asias* [The genocide of the Greeks and Armenians of Asia Minor] (Athens, 1988).

Pallis, A.A., *Greece's Anatolian Venture and After: A Survey of the Diplomatic and Political Aspects of the Greek Expedition to Asia Minor (1915–1922)*(London: Methuen, 1937).

_____, *Anadromi sto prosfygiko zitima* [The refugee question in retrospect] (Athens, 1963).

_____, *I andallagi ton plethismon* [The exchange of population] (Athens, 1933).

_____. *Statistiki meleti peri ton fyletikon metanasteuseon Makedonias kai Thrakis tin periodo 1912–1924* [A statistical study concerning the racial migration in Macedonia and Thrace in the years 1912–1924] (Athens, 1925).

Pentzopoulos, Dimitri, *The Balkan Exchange of Minorities and Its Impact upon Greece* (Paris and the Hague: Mouton, 1962).

Petsalis-Diomidis, Nikos, *Greece at the Peace Conference, 1919* (Thessaloniki: Institute for Balkan Studies, 1978).

Protonotarios, Athanasios V., *To prosfigikon problema* [The refugee problem] (Athens, 1929).

Psomiades, Harry J., *The Eastern Question: The Last Phase. A Study in Greek-Turkish Diplomacy* (Thessaloniki: Institute for Balkan Studies, 1968).

_____, T.A. Couloumbis and J.A. Petropulos, *Foreign Interference in Greek Politics: An Historical Perspective* (New York: Pella Publishing Co., 1976).

Seferiades, Stelios, *L'échange des populations* (Paris: Hachette, 1929).

Smith, Michael Llewellyn, *Ionian Vision, Greece in Asia Minor, 1919–1922* (London: A. Lane, 1973).

Sonyel, Salahi, *Turkish Diplomacy, 1918–1923* (London: Sage, 1975).

Svolopoulos, Constantine, *I apofasi gia tin ypohreotiki antallagi ton plithismon metaxi Ellados kai Turkias* [The decision for the complusory exchange of populations between Greece and Turkey] (Thessaloniki: Etairia Makedonikon Spoudon, 1981).

Toynbee, Arnold J., *The Western Question in Greece and Turkey* (London: Constable and Co., 1922).

Tounta-Fergadi, Arete, *To prosfygiko daneio tou 1924* [The refugee loan of 1924] (Thessaloniki: Parateretes, 1986).

Türkgeldi, A., *Moudros ve Mudanya Mütarekeleri Tarihi* [History of the Moudros and Mudanya Armistices] (Ankara: Güney Matbaacilik ve Gazetecilik, 1948).

Yildirim, Onur, *Diplomats and Refugees: Mapping the Turco-Greek Exchange of Populations, 1922–1924* (Ph.D. dissertation, Princeton University, 2002).

Zapantis, Andrew L., *Greek-Soviet Relations, 1917–1941* (Boulder: East European Monographs, 1982).

*Articles*

Allis, William T., "Jennings of Smyrna," *Scribner's* (August 1928): 230–235.

Aralov, S.I. "In the Turkey of Atatürk" *International Affairs* [Moscow] 8 (August 1960): 81–87.

Chater, Melville, "History's Greatest Trek," *The National Geographic Magazine* 48, no. 5 (November 1925): 533–590.

Dakin, Douglas, "The Greek Army in Thrace and the Conference of Lausanne," in *Greece and Great Britain during World War I* (Thessaloniki: Institute for Balkan Studies, 1985), pp. 210–232.

———, "Lord Curzon's Policy Towards Greece," in *Essays in Memory of Basil Laourdas,* (Thessaloniki: Institute for Balkan Studies, 1975), pp. 539–550.

Davison, Roderic H., "Turkish Diplomacy from Mudros to Lausanne," in G.A. Craig and Felix Gilbert, eds. *The Diplomats, 1919–1939* (Princeton: Princeton University Press, 1953), pp. 172–209.

Haidar, Alaeddine, "Le problèm de l'échange des populations," *Aurore* [Paris] (October 30, 1922): 1.

Hassiotis, I.K., "Armenians," in Richard Clogg, ed., *Minorities in Greece: Aspects of a Plural Society* (London: Hurst & Company, 1998), pp. 94–111.

Koufa, Kalliopi K. and Constantine Svolopoulos, "The Compulsory Exchange of Populations between Greece and Turkey: The Settlement of the Minority Questions at the Conference of Lausanne, 1923, and its Impact on Greek-Turkish Relations," in *Ethnic Groups in International Relations,* Vol. 5, edited by Paul Smith in collaboration with Kalliopi Koufa and Arnold Suppan (New York: New York University Press, 1991).

Nicolopoulos, John, "The Testimony of Michail Vassilievich Frunze Concerning the Tragedy of Pontic Hellenism," *Journal of Modern Hellenism* no. 4 (1987): 37–53.

Okyar, Osman, "Turco-British Relations in the Inter-War Period: Fethi Okyar's Mission to London," in William Hale and Ali Ihsan Bagis, editors, *Four Centuries of Turco-British Relations, Studies in Diplomatic, Economic and Cultural Affairs* (North Humberside: Eothen Press, 1984), pp. 62–79.

Pallis, A.A., "The Exchange of Populations in the Balkans," *The Nineteenth Century* 47 (March 1925): 1–8.

———, "Racial Migration in the Balkans during the Years 1912–1914," *Geographical Journal* 66, no. 4 (October 1925): 52–60.

Petropulos, John A., "The Compulsory Exchange of Populations: Greek-Turkish Peacemaking, 1922–1930," *Byzantine and Modern Greek Studies* 2 (1976): 135–160.

Petsalis-Diomidis, Nikos, "Hellenism in Southern Russia and the Ukranian Campaign: Their Effects on the Pontos Question, 1919," *Balkan Studies* 13, no. 2 (1971): 228–229, 250–258.

Psomiades, Harry J., "The American Near East Relief (NER) and the Megali Catastrophe in 1922," *Journal of Modern Hellenism* 19 (Winter 2001): 135–150.

———, "The Diplomacy of Theodoros Pangalos, 1925–1926," *Balkan Studies* 13, no. 1 (1972): 1–16.

———, "Eastern Thrace and the Armistice of Mudanya, October 3–11, 1922," *Journal of Modern Hellenism* 17–18 (Winter 2000–2001): 1–67.

————, "Fridtjof Nansen and the Greek Refugee Problem, September-November 1922," *Deltio* [Athens] 16 (2009): 287–346.

Shuttleworth, D.I., "Turkey: From the Armistice to Peace," *The Journal of the Central Asian Society* 11, no. 1 (1924): 60–62.

Sveen, Asie, "Fridtjof Nansen: Scientist and Humanitarian," March 15, 2001 in Nobelprize.org.

Svolopoulos, Constantine and Koufa, Halliopi, "The Compulsory Exchange of Populations between Greece and Turkey: The Settlement of Minority Questions at the Conference of Lausanne, 1923, and Its Impact on Greek-Turkish Relations," in Paul Smith, ed., *Ethnic Groups in International Relations,* Vol. V (New York: New York University Press, 1991), pp. 268–280.

Tounda-Fergadi, Arete, "L'histoire de l'emprunt accorde pour les réfugiés de 1924," *Balkan Studies* [Thessaloniki], 24, no. 1 (1983): 89–105.

*Periodicals and Newspapers*

*Balkan Studies,* Thessaloniki
*Bulletin périodique de la presse grecque,* Paris, 1922–1925
*Bulletin périodique de la presse turque,* Paris, 1922–1925
*Oriente Moderno,* Rome, 1922–1925
*Revue Internationale de la Croix-Rouge,* Geneva, 1920–1930


*Daily Telegraph.* London
*Kathemerini*
*Le Messager d'Athènes*
*The Times.* London.
*The New York Times*
*To Vima*

# Index

*Note to Index*: An "n" after a page number denotes a note on that page.

# Maps

Map 1. The Eastern Mediterranean

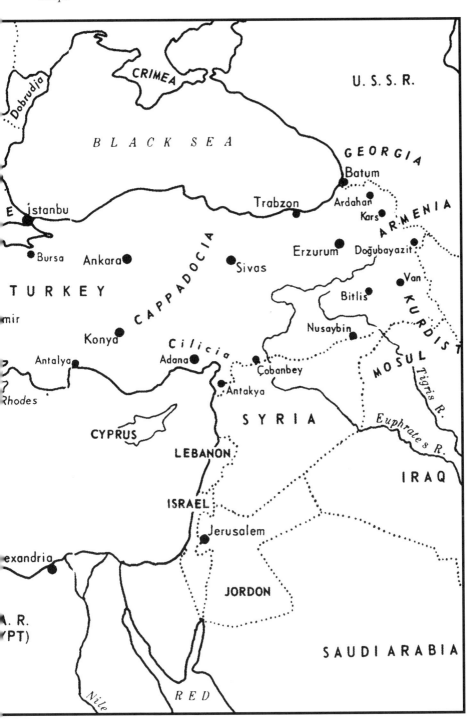

## Map 3. The Greek-Turkish Frontier in Thrace

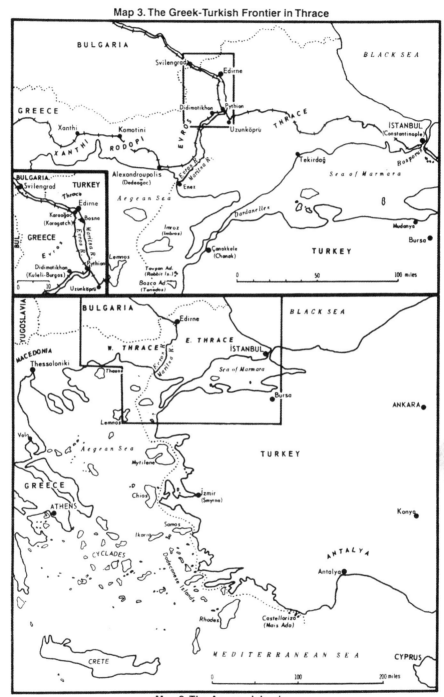

Map 2. The Aegean Islands